Never Take No
For An Answer

Jan 1990

D0569240

Never Take No For An Answer

A Guide to Successful Negotiation

Samfrits Le Poole

Kogan
Page

First published in 1987 by
Kogan Page Limited
120 Pentonville Road
London N1 9JN

British Library Cataloguing in Publication Data
Le Poole, Samfrits
    Never take no for an answer: a guide to
    successful negotiation.
    1. Negotiation
    I. Title
    158.5   BF637.N4

    ISBN 1-85091-314-5
    ISBN 1-85091-431-1 Pbk

Printed and bound in Great Britain by
Billing and Sons Ltd, Worcester.

To Macha, Bob, Frank and Jaap —
my favourite people in this world

Contents

Preface   **9**

1. The Good and Not So Good Negotiator   **11**
Qualities 11; Flaws 13; The ideal negotiator 15

2. The Negotiating Process   **17**
The negotiator's dilemmas 18; Stages of the
negotiating process 20; Nature of negotiations 22;
Enough is enough 25; Who should go first? 26

3. On Preparation   **29**
What kind of negotiations? 30; Win/lose or win/win? 30;
Is agreement a must? 31; Bilateral or multilateral
negotiations? 32; Is the opponent internally divided? 32;
Will there be knock-on effects? 33; Is ratification
required? 33; Are the negotiations private or public? 34;
Can the agreement be enforced? 34; Will the other
negotiator remain involved afterwards? 35; Which
parties are facing which deadlines? 36; Does your
opponent really want an agreement? 36; The checklist
for preparation 36; Fact-finding 37; Review of past
negotiations 39; The issues 40; Target — opening
position — walk-away point 40; Best alternative 42;
Arguments 43; Concessions 43; Strengths and
weaknesses 44; The opponent's vantage point 44;
Strategy and tactics 45; Agenda 45; Dress rehearsal 47

4. Aspirations and Concessions   **49**
Aspirations 49; The do's and dont's of
concession-making 52

5. Deadlocks   **59**

Means to break an impasse 60

6. The Role of Time   **63**

Rush deals 64; Deadlines 64; Negotiating abroad 65;
Some tips on timing 67; Telephone negotiating 67

7. Some Tactics   **69**

Last minute escalation 69; Fading beauty 70; Good
guy/bad guy 71; Take it or leave it 73; Limited
authority 75; Lock-in 77; 'Pardon my French' 79;
Intimidation 80; Emotional outbursts 81; Advance
man 81; Information from heaven 81

Conclusion   **83**

Bibliography   **85**

Index   **89**

Preface

Almost all books on negotiating are either of the how-to-bargain-for-
a-free-tie-if-you-buy-a-new-suit variety or highly theoretical, replete
with mathematics and game theory. This book limits itself to the
practical ins and outs of negotiating without, I hope, being simplistic.
Although it covers all areas of practical importance it has been kept
brief and concise. It is meant to serve as a handbook, to be used both
by the professional negotiator and by everybody else who once in a
while has to negotiate. And who does not? By handbook I mean a
book that will not only be read once or twice but also serves as
reference before, during and after negotiations.

No book can in and by itself make the reader an accomplished
negotiator. But this book certainly has the ambition to make the
reader a better negotiator. It intends to do so by enhancing the
reader's insight into what is happening at the negotiating table and by
providing numerous practical suggestions, recommendations,
warnings, do's and don'ts.

Two caveats. This book deals only with commercial negotiating,
not with negotiating between diplomats. That is an entirely separate
subject about which some good books have been written, like Fred C
Iklé's *How Nations Negotiate*.

Furthermore, I'm fully aware that all the rules, precepts and
suggestions in this book have been formulated broadly. Everything I
say and recommend is, in my opinion, generally true, but subject to
exceptions. In negotiating hardly anything applies always. An all-
round negotiator has to be flexible, able to adjust to the specific
requirements of the specific negotiations he is conducting with a
specific opponent in specific circumstances. To almost every
statement I could have added qualifiers like 'generally', 'with many
exceptions', 'as a general rule' etc. Accuracy would have been
enhanced but readability severely impaired. So I have chosen the
lesser evil of broad generalizations, assuming that no reader will even

think of rigidly applying every rule and every recommendation every time he or she is involved in negotiations.

Throughout this book, the personal pronoun 'he' has been adopted solely to avoid repetitious use of the phrase 'he or she'. Women do, of course, negotiate in business more and more, and should always be considered as equally included wherever the context permits.

The Good and Not So Good Negotiator

Why is it important to know the profile of the good and not so good negotiator? First, know thyself! Once at a seminar about negotiating, which I gave, a man came to me and said, 'This is a very expensive seminar, but to me it has been worth every penny.' Expecting a very complimentary explanation, I asked him why. All he said was: 'I learned that I was not born to negotiate; I never will any more and that will save me a lot of money and frustration.' Second, it helps to be able to recognize the accomplished and the flawed negotiator. If you negotiate with somebody who clearly loves to be liked, make it clear to him that you're prepared to like him forever . . . provided he gives in a little bit more. If your opponent almost seems to ignore your objections and rejections, do not get annoyed, do not assume the man is deaf and blind. It may be that you're dealing with a very persistent negotiator who knows, from experience, that by persevering he can turn many noes into maybe's and many maybe's into yesses. If your opponent talks too much or shows frequent signs of impatience, you can assume that he's neither experienced nor overly competent. If he seems constantly to be able to read your mind or your non-verbal messages, the reverse is true.

One purpose of this book is to make the reader a better, preferably a good negotiator. But what is a good negotiator? He should have as many of the following qualities as possible.

Qualities

Patience is an absolute requirement for a negotiator. Negotiating can be a very drawn out and even boring exercise. One has to be able to endure endless repetitions, digressions and irrelevancies without giving in to the very human urge to conclude the matter as soon as possible. All too often, unnecessary concessions are made because the

11

negotiator wants to move on, and less than optimal deals are accepted because above all else he wants to bring the whole thing to a close.

Patience plays an important role not only in the negotiations themselves, but also in the preparation for them, quite often an elaborate and time-consuming process. A negotiator should have both the know-how and the self-discipline for careful planning.

Negotiations are not always dull affairs. Far from it. They can be very exciting and stressful. A good negotiator, therefore, is able to think on his feet and remain cool under stress.

A negotiator should be open-minded, flexible and able to put himself in his opponent's shoes. You can only communicate with somebody whom you understand, whether you agree with him or not.

Inventiveness and creativity are often required to avoid or break deadlocks, to find alternative approaches and solutions, to create a deal which is best for both parties.

Perseverance is important. A negotiator should be a go-getter.

Because he will hear many more noes than yesses in the course of negotiations, he should not easily take no for an answer. He should also be ambitious in the sense of setting high goals and standards for himself.

A good negotiator is self-confident and robust in the face of criticism. Again and again he will be told how stupid, how unreasonable, how devious he is. He cannot afford to be affected by accusations made in an opportunist spirit.

Listening is essential. And by listening I mean listening well, actively, creatively, with understanding. This is a rather rare talent, but in negotiating your ears are as important as your tongue.

A good negotiator not only listens but also observes well. He is perceptive and skilful in reading cues, in picking up non-verbal messages. As long as we still negotiate with human beings, understanding of human nature is essential. A negotiator cannot afford to be naive.

A good negotiator knows how to perceive and exploit power. He realizes who is in the driver's seat and when that happens to be him, he knows how to capitalize fully on that comfortable position. He is also constantly aware of the way the balance of power shifts. In commercial negotiating he should, of course, also have good business judgement.

A natural inclination to take charge and grasp the initiative is an important attribute. Bur first of all a negotiator has to be in charge of himself. Self-control is essential.

An analytical mind helps. Specifically, a negotiator should be able to distinguish between major and minor issues. All too often tremendous battles are fought about minor issues, while major issues are conceded with no more than a shrug of the shoulders. And too many negotiations deadlock on issues which in the final analysis are details.

As we have seen, the ultimate goal of the negotiator is to make his opponent do what he wants. So being persuasive is crucial. It certainly helps if a negotiator is courteous, personable and tactful. His opponents will feel more comfortable with him and will be less reluctant to give in. Often people react more to the messenger than to the message. Personal qualities are of particular importance when you have to relay an unpleasant message or when you have to take a rigid attitude.

The three Rs: a negotiator should be reasonable, rational and realistic. Unnecessary to elaborate on that.

I have dealt with numerous good negotiators. None of them had all these talents and abilities. The more the better, but if you have most of them to a not insignificant degree you are ahead of many of the people who negotiate a lot. Provided that you have none of the flaws which handicap a negotiator. And what are these?

Flaws

The worst trait a negotiator can possess is an eagerness to please. Wanting to be liked is normal, but in the course of negotiating you will have to displease a lot of people a lot of times. If you find that difficult, do not negotiate.

Similarly, it's a noble human inclination to try to be reasonable all the time. Some people are not even able to be unreasonable. But, whether he likes it or not, a negotiator cannot avoid being unreasonable on occasion.

A naive and over-trusting negotiator will be liable to be eaten alive. As we have seen, play-acting, misrepresentations and deceit are elements of the negotiating process which are all too common. Distrust is a bad basis for negotiations, but a healthy dose of scepticism is indispensible for a negotiator.

Rigid people who think in terms of reasonable and unreasonable, right and wrong, should not negotiate. They do not understand that most things in life are relative. They lack the flexibility to take a look at issues through the eyes of the opponent. A negotiator should always keep in mind that, were he sitting at the other end of the table, he

13

would talk differently. Bertrand Russell said: 'It matters little what you believe, as long as you do not altogether believe it.' That's what I believe — altogether!

The way to be taken advantage of in negotiation is to let your emotions loose. Although emotions can sometimes be used effectively, an emotional person with too much temperament should not negotiate.

Other negatives are: a tendency to be quarrelsome, argumentative or belligerent (which almost forces people to argue back and disagree with you), a lust for self-promotion, a need to score points continuously and a lack of self-knowledge and self-criticism.

Finally, a negotiator should not be uncomfortable with uncertainty. As we shall see, negotiations take place within a zone of not knowing, where risks are difficult to assess, where you have to rely on educated and sometimes not so educated guesses, where you have to deal with a variety of unknowns and dilemmas. Some of the most able and intelligent people are frightened by uncertainties and ambiguities. As long as things are certain, they can deal with them, even if they are bad or complex. Uncertainties baffle or scare them. Those people should not negotiate.

I once bought a small aeroplane for an amazingly low price (£10,000). Much later I met the seller again and he started to talk about our negotiations. I mentioned that I had been pleasantly surprised by the bargain. He told me that when he decided to sell the plane, he had aimed for £14,000. That was why his asking price had been £15,000. The absolute minimum he wanted to get was £10,000. Moreover, he had very much wanted to sell the plane before he went on holiday six weeks later. It had been on the market for two days when I came along and offered, after some bargaining, £10,000.

That price was very disappointing for him. But, as he told me, suddenly all kinds of 'what ifs' started to crop up. What if I walked out if he didn't accept my offer right away? What if other potential buyers should offer even less? What if nobody else turned up? It might be that my offer was barely acceptable but, by accepting it nevertheless, he got two things: some money and certainty. Because he overvalued certainty he was willing to concede heavily on money. And because he overpaid for certainty, he ended up with an unnecessarily poor deal. Of course there was some risk involved in not accepting my offer at his absolute minimum but, assuming that the target price of £14,000 was realistic, and in view of the fact that I was the first bidder and that much time was left before the deadline he had set himself, a good negotiator would have taken that calculated risk.

The ideal negotiator

The desire to define the ideal negotiator is an old one. In his delightful essay, published in 1716, 'On the Manner of Negotiating with Princes — on the Uses of Diplomacy, the Choice of Ministers and Envoys and the Personal Qualities Necessary for Success in Missions Abroad', de Callières gives this description: 'The ideal negotiator has a quick mind, but unlimited patience; he knows how to be modest but assertive, how to mislead without being a liar, how to inspire trust without himself trusting others, how to charm others without succumbing to their charms, and he possesses plenty of money and a beautiful wife so that he can remain indifferent to all temptations of riches and women.' A perceptive definition, for sure, but who fits the bill?

The Negotiating Process

I have long abandoned my search for an all-encompassing definition of 'negotiating'. Its broad, intangible and diverse character makes this the ultimate exercise in futility. It can be helpful, however, to make the negotiating process somewhat transparent by breaking it down into a few characteristic features.

Negotiations take place between two or more parties with some common and some conflicting interests, but with the same purpose: to arrive at an agreement. If they negotiate well, they also have a longer-term purpose: to engender a mutual lasting spirit to live up to the deal. They constantly keep in mind that it's one thing to arrive at an agreement but quite another to get the agreement implemented. The ultimate goal of negotiating is not to obtain a piece of paper with some signatures but to get certain things done. The end result of negotiations should be a sincere commitment by all parties to faithfully, loyally and honestly live up to a fair, unambiguous deal with which they are all satisfied.

Parties to negotiations are totally dependent on each other. However 'right', reasonable or powerful one is, so long as the opponent does not sign, there is no deal ('opponent' will be used throughout this book to denote the person with whom one negotiates, although for many negotiating situations this is an unduly harsh and antagonistic term). Both parties have veto power. Even in a very lopsided situation where one party is much more dependent on the other than vice versa, the stronger party needs the weaker one for acceptance of the deal.

Give and take is inherent in negotiating. A one-way street does not lead to agreement. And I'm not only thinking about concessions and counter-concessions but also, for example, about exchange of information. Progress in negotiations is not made unless both parties provide relevant information to each other.

Most negotiations involve some measure of play-acting, manipulation and strategic misrepresentations. Even outright lying, albeit unacceptable, is not uncommon. Incidentally, two effective ways to detect lying are to ask your opponent questions to which you already know the answer and to ask him the same question more than once at different times and in different contexts so that you can check whether you get the same answer each time.

The negotiator's dilemmas

The most prevalent characteristic of negotiating is uncertainty. The negotiator constantly has to feel his way around among dilemmas. He's continuously beset by question marks. He hardly ever knows, most of the time he can only guess and wonder. That makes negotiating challenging, exciting and frustrating at the same time.

Let's take a look at some of the dilemmas a negotiator is confronted with all the time.

The dependency dilemma

The negotiator is out to serve his own interests, but he cannot disregard the interests of his opponent. Otherwise there will be no agreement. For purely opportunistic reasons, his natural egoism has to be tempered. But to what extent?

The power perception dilemma

Who is in the driver's seat? Is the opponent's position as strong as the self-confidence which he radiates suggests? Does the opponent know about your weaknesses and time constraints? Frequently negotiators underestimate their power or, more correctly, overestimate the power of their opponent. The reason is that they are very aware of their own weaknesses, restraints and deadlines, but unaware of those on the part of the opponent, although they should know from experience that the opponent most probably has some.

The mind-reading dilemma

Does the opponent really mean what he's saying? As pointed out, play-acting, exaggerating, misleading etc are integral parts of the negotiating process and the negotiator has to wonder constantly whether or not he should believe his opponent.

The information dilemma

How close should you keep your cards to your chest? Which information should be kept secret, which can be disclosed? When and to what extent?

The concession dilemma

When are which concessions called for?

The attitudinal dilemma

Should you play hardball? Or should you be flexible? When is a change in attitude called for?

The impasse dilemma

Is an impasse imminent? Would that be a disaster?

The trust dilemma

The negotiator who is too trusting will constantly be taken advantage of, but mere mistrust cannot be the basis for fruitful negotiations. The odds that two parties who do not trust each other will reach agreement are small and the odds that such an agreement will be implemented without complications are even smaller. But to what extent can this specific opponent be trusted?

The authority dilemma

The negotiator himself deems the deal reasonable and acceptable, but wonders whether he can sell it to his boss, his members or his client.

The self-evaluation dilemma

How did you do? Did you not give in too much? Did you get the best possible deal? One of the most annoying aspects of negotiating is that it is hardly ever possible to evaluate your own performance. What should be the yardstick? The status quo? The mere fact that the agreement is better than the status quo does not imply that it is as good as possible. The absolute minimum which you set yourself prior to the negotiations? Again, the end result might be acceptable, but could it not have been more acceptable? And even if you accomplished everything you wanted to, it does not follow automatically that you have negotiated well. It may be that your targets were too low or that the outcome was more determined by the ineptness of your opponent than by your own acumen.

Because so many uncertainties play such a decisive role in negotiations and the outcome is so largely based on assumptions and guesses, educated or not, it is unavoidable that almost every agreement falls short of the best result, which, with the benefit of hindsight, could have been obtained. Almost always a better deal for both parties would have been possible. This phenomenon made Howard Raiffa (in *The Art and Science of Negotiation* — a very good book, but of little use in actual practice) theorize about a 'contract embellisher': somebody to whom both parties before the start of negotiations separately confide their needs, perceptions, priorities, expectations, constraints, targets, absolute minima, acceptable concessions etc, and who, after a binding agreement has been signed, proposes to both parties an agreement that for both of them would be better than the one they agreed on. It is then up to both parties to decide whether or not to accept this supposedly objectively better agreement. If not, the agreement they negotiated and signed stands.

Stages of the negotiating process

Preparation

This stage is of such importance that Chapter 3 is entirely dedicated to it.

The negotiation sessions

These form the second stage.

Negotiating sessions start with an *orientation phase*. Parties exchange information about their companies or their backgrounds. Individual members of negotiating teams are introduced. The negotiators engage in small talk and pleasantries. They try to break the ice and get a feel for each other. Personal relationships start to take shape.

In more formal negotiations opening statements are made. And in many negotiations the agenda and ground rules (matters like length of sessions, frequency of recesses, target date for conclusion, contact with media) are discussed. This can be a very short, superficial discussion, but it can also be a separate negotiation process prior to the real negotiations themselves. Sometimes disagreement about the agenda or ground rules aborts negotiations before they get the chance to take off. An important part of the orientation phase is the determination of the authority of the negotiators. Do they have the final say or will everything they accept be subject to approval by somebody else? If so, by whom?

In the next phase parties *position* themselves and *argue* their case. All issues are reviewed in some detail. The negotiators explain and defend their opening positions, question and attack those of their opponents, probe for soft spots, try to get an idea about what the opponent is doing, wanting, expecting, striving for. This phase is often characterized by rhetorical fireworks and psychological warfare.

In the third phase the *search for solutions* starts. Information is exchanged. Concessions are made. The rhetoric is toned down. Parties move towards consensus. The contours of the agreement emerge.

Often negotiations go through a *crisis phase*, in which deadlines loom and deadlocks occur. This phase can mean the end of the negotiations, but also the catharsis, opening the way to the *settlement phase*, in which the last, often thorniest issues are solved, agreement is reached, a written contract is drafted and reviewed, finishing touches are applied and sometimes last minute problems arising out of second thoughts or misunderstandings are solved.

If somebody else has to consent to the agreement, the entire process is concluded with a *ratification phase*. This phase can require further negotiations in case the transaction is not fully approved. Later on we will see that this phase lends itself to all kinds of games.

Monitoring

As a final stage, the agreement is monitored. When the agreement is implemented it often appears that not every contingency has been forseen, discussed and provided for during the negotiations. Unexpected complications pop up. Decisions and commitments which were made appear to be unworkable or unreasonably burdensome for one of the parties. Adjustment is required; in other words, renegotiation. Even if you can legally hold your opponent to the terms of the agreement, it's generally in your own interest to renegotiate if it turns out that living up to the deal would be an unexpected burden for him. Apart from the fact that tomorrow the roles might be reversed, you are only asking for trouble, marginal compliance, delays and quality shortcomings if you force the other party to live up reluctantly to a deal which he for good reasons considers unfair and lopsided.

Nature of negotiations

Negotiations should not be a debate. And what do they turn into often? A debate! Parties make statements, take positions, defend their own point of view, attack their opponent's position, emphasize how right they are and how wrong their opponents are etc. Whatever satisfaction such debates may give, minds are hardly ever changed by them. The negotiator's aim should be to influence, to persuade, to convince his opponent. Convince of what? It helps to convince your opponent that your position is reasonable because it is easier for him to accept a reasonable proposition than to accept one reluctantly which he finds repulsive. But the ultimate goal of the negotiator is to make his opponent understand that it is in his own interest to acquiesce.

A number of techniques for persuasion and, more broadly, for fruitful discussion are at issue in all negotiations and it is useful to go over them.

Listening

Listen well, actively, with understanding. Easily said, but apparently not so easily done. Many people cannot listen. The best they can do is to keep silent for a while, waiting until it is their turn to speak again, in the meantime thinking about what they are going to say. Do not talk too much. The more your opponent talks, the more you learn. Listen, as it were, between the lines and to the fine print. To the nuances, the intonation, the choice of words. Make a mental note if somebody who has been saying all the time 'absolutely not' suddenly says 'I'm afraid not', or 'possibly' instead of 'probably', or 'I believe' instead of 'I know', or 'I prefer' instead of 'I demand'.

Good listening should go arm in arm with sharp observing. Watch your opponent while he is talking. Be alert for non-verbal clues. Many people have no problem in making statements which they don't believe in but give their disbelief away by their demeanour.

Show your opponent that you listened to him by reacting to what he said. Two monologues do not make a dialogue, and it is only in the course of a dialogue that minds may change.

When you talk, do not talk too long in one stretch and keep in mind that by and large the end of a presentation is remembered better than the beginning and the beginning better than the middle. You want your opponent to listen well to you and the shorter and more concisely you speak, the higher the odds that he will do so.

A few quotes illustrate the point well: 'Essence of a good

presentation: have a good beginning and a good end and keep them close together' and 'Stand up to be seen — speak up to be heard — shut up to be liked' and 'If people would listen to themselves more, they would talk less.' Remember the devastating words Disraeli once spoke after he had suffered through a long speech of a political opponent: 'We have forgotten the beginning of your speech, we did not pay any attention to the middle and nothing has given us pleasure in it except the end.'

To every rule there is an exception. Sometimes it might serve a purpose to overwhelm your opponent with words: 'If you cannot convince them, confuse them' or, less elegantly, 'If you cannot dazzle them with brilliance, baffle them with bullshit.'

In a roundabout way the importance of listening was stressed by the Dutch captain of industry, Frits Philips, who often admonished his negotiators not to listen to their opponents because, by listening, they would run the risk of being convinced. Of course, he hardly ever really had to negotiate: more often than not he was in a position to simply dictate.

Part of listening is not interrupting. Interrupting annoys and, more importantly, is not effective because what is said by way of interruption is hardly ever listened to. The interruptee either talks on or merely waits for an opportunity to pick up where you forced him to leave off.

Do not be in a hurry to bring up your views. Wait till you have your opponent's full viewpoint. And do not jump to conclusions before he has had the opportunity to make his entire case. Often people address presumed, instead of real, viewpoints.

Make an effort to understand why your opponent is saying what he's saying. Only if you understand him, whether you agree with him or not, can you influence him. It's entirely normal that the guy at the other end of the table is also at the other end of the argument. Take a look at the issues through his eyes. Realize that his interests and his vantage point are different from yours. Put yourself in his shoes.

Choice of emphasis

A good way to create an atmosphere which is conducive to consensus is to emphasize similarities between your opponent's position and your own and to understate the differences. If both parties realize they have quite a bit in common, they are more inclined to bridge the gap between them.

To be effective in discussions you have to phrase your messages in such a way that the odds for eliciting a favourable response are enhanced. Often what you say is less important than how you say it. The melody can be more important than the words. A diplomat, well-known for his negotiating acumen, attributed his success to his talent to send somebody to hell in such a way that he was really looking forward to the trip!

If you have to give your opponent a negative or unpleasant message it is best to give your explanations and reasons first and only thereafter the negative conclusion. If you start with the latter, the chances are that your opponent is so disappointed, amazed or angry that he will hardly pay attention to your explanation.

Don't try to be complete and exhaustive. Concentrate on your stronger points and arguments. Otherwise you invite your opponent to attack you on the weaker ones, which can shift the momentum of the discussion and undermine the strength of your position. As a corollary of this, try to zero in on the weaker points of your opponent's position; force him to spend time, energy and attention on defending them — to the detriment of his stronger points.

Questions

Questions are pivotal in a discussion. Ask a lot and listen to the answers. I'm always amazed how easily people let opponents get away with ignoring questions or with evasive or irrelevant answers. If you do not receive a to-the-point answer to your question, it might be because the question has been misunderstood, but more likely it is a sign that your opponent does not have a satisfactory answer. And that can be an important clue for you.

You yourself should never answer a question unless you clearly understand that question. Don't try to look smarter than you are. Nothing is less smart than giving the wrong answer to a misunderstood question.

Of course some questions do not deserve answers. If you decide that that is the case, tell your opponent that you will leave his question unanswered. And often there's no reason not to tell him why.

Acceptance time

Chester Karrass introduced the concept of acceptance time. Allow your opponent time to digest your ideas and proposals. A negative reaction to a new idea or proposal is only natural. Do not give up or become impatient. Your opponent needs and deserves time to understand and appreciate them. So if you come up with a new idea, especially if it is a creative, somewhat unusual idea, do not let an initially negative reaction discourage you. Rather than trying to rebut the negative response, explain and re-explain; or put your idea on the back burner for a while to bring it up again later when it is no longer new, revolutionary and scary to your opponent.

Actions speak louder than words

Finally, precedents, reputations, track records etc have persuasive value. They can substantiate or cast doubt on whatever you are saying. If you have a track record of being honest and reliable, you will need less effort to persuade your opponent to trust and believe you. If you are a known bluffer it will be tough for you to convince somebody that you are not bluffing, even when — for a change — you are not.

Self-evaluation

It would be worthwhile, on completion of your next negotiations, to re-read the last pages in order to check where you stood in relation to their suggestions. It will help you to evaluate your own performance. Make this self-evaluation a habit for a while and soon you will do better and therefore be a better negotiator.

Enough is enough

Talking about convincing, let's take a look at one crucial stage of the game. When are negotiations ripe for conclusion? Only if two requirements are met. First, the deal you are proposing should be better for your opponent than no deal at all. Second, he should be convinced that you are not prepared to improve the deal for him; in other words, that you are not going to make more concessions. If one of those two requirements is not met, your opponent is not yet prepared to refrain from further bargaining. If he realizes that you will not make more concessions, but he would be better off without an agreement than with the one you're offering, he will not accept your offer. On the other hand, if he likes your last offer but hopes that further bargaining will improve the deal, he will also continue to negotiate (at least this is generally the situation; sometimes a negotiator is not bent on getting the best possible deal and is willing to accept an agreement, although by pressing on he could probably get more concessions). So how can you make it clear to him that your bottom line has been reached?

The most straightforward way is to say so explicitly. But do it in absolute terms. Make it clear that you are serious. Just saying 'That's it, I will not go any further' is not enough. Those and similar words are used too often, too routinely. Commit yourself, as it were, not to go any further.

Show your opponent that you have lost interest in the discussion. Merely repeat yourself. Do not come up with new arguments and rebuttals. Use non-verbal means. Convey boredom and indifference by the way you are talking, sitting and behaving.

Prove to your opponent, if possible, that an agreement which would require further concessions would not make sense from your point of view. You can do so by showing him better alternative offers open to you, if you have them.

Emotional outbursts can be a good means to make your opponent feel that he is going too far, that he is overdoing it, that he should stop here and now. Get angry, in a controlled fashion, at your opponent's demand for more concessions, exude indignation, pound the table. I once negotiated with a debtor of a client about the repayment of his debt in instalments. After a while, the debtor, a huge, fifty-year-old man, started to weep. I still do not know whether he was acting or not, but I do know that I felt that I had gone as far as I could, probably even too far, and I did not push the man any further.

All these means can be effective. But *the* way to give your opponent the message that he should not press for more is to take back a concession which you have made already. Not everybody agrees that this is honourable and it depends somewhat on the circumstances, but in general I am of the opinion, without hesitation, that every concession or agreement on an individual item of a larger agenda can be withdrawn at any time before final agreement on the entire package. Nothing is more persuasive in making it clear to an opponent that not only will he not get anywhere with trying to push for further concessions, but that in fact he will be worse off by doing so.

Who should go first?

Who should be the first to disclose his position, to spell out his demands, to make an offer? You or your opponent? Both possibilities have their pros and cons. The advantages of being first are that you take the initiative, that you set the tone of the discussions, that your position becomes the focal point of the negotiations. The disadvantages are threefold. Possibly you do not have an inkling of what your opponent expects or desires. You might therefore start off with a proposal which is much more attractive than he expected and would have asked for, if he had started. In that case he will raise his demands. Moreover, your opponent might limit himself to reacting to your position without revealing his. And, finally, the one who opens the bidding is generally expected to be also the first one to make a concession. In the normal course of negotiations, A sets forth his position, B replies to A's statement and explains his position, whereupon A replies to B's statement and makes the first concession.

By and large the disadvantages prevail over the advantages. Let your opponent start. However, if you want to shock your opponent with your opening offer you should go first. We will elaborate on this concept later, but sometimes it is a good approach to start negotiations with an extreme, although not entirely unrealistic, demand. Such a demand often makes the opponent water down his opening position even before he has had the chance to reveal it.

Another situation in which the advantage of taking the initiative prevails over all the disadvantages of making the opening move occurs when negotiations are conducted on the basis of a rather detailed document, like a draft agreement. The draftsman is in a position to take charge of the discussion. He enumerates and frames the issues. He can subtly phrase every clause to his advantage. He can insert give-aways — demands and positions which he knows will be unacceptable to the opponent and which can be conceded without any problem but, the hope is, at a price. In short, drafting the document which will serve as the basis for the negotiations provides the opportunity to put the opponent right away on the defensive. I always consider letting the opponent incur the expense of having his solicitor draft the proposed agreement, the ultimate example of penny-wisdom, pound-foolishness.

Chapter 3

On Preparation

Failing to plan is planning to fail!

Nothing is more important in negotiating than exhaustive, to-the-point preparation. This implies not only that you have to be willing to take time to prepare, but also that you must know how to prepare. Awareness that you have to do your homework and willingness to do it do not suffice. You also have to know what your homework consists of.

I know of many instances where an experienced and able but unprepared negotiator met a less experienced and less able, but much better prepared opponent. Invariably the latter came out ahead.

Some people do not prepare sufficiently because they think they will do better if they fly by the seat of their pants. They are in for many crash landings. The more common reason for inadequate preparation, however, is lack of time. If you really lack time to prepare, you should not negotiate. Preparation is not a luxury to be indulged in, time permitting. It's an integral and crucial part of the negotiating process itself. You would not want to negotiate in Chinese, because you could neither understand nor react adequately to what was being said. Neither would you want to negotiate about a subject you were not familiar with, because you would not be able to talk sense. Well, even in less obvious cases, if you do not prepare well for negotiations, you will be equally unable to react adequately or to talk sense.

In order to make sure that all matters which have to be considered in the course of preparation are included, that nothing is overlooked, a checklist should be used. I will present my checklist, which has served me well over the course of years, but everybody can draw up his own checklist according to his own views, preferences, and experiences. Specific negotiations (like those about collective labour contracts) require specific checklists. But in all cases use a checklist!

What kind of negotiations?

Before going through your checklist, you have to ask yourself what kind of negotiations you are preparing for, because there are all kinds of negotiations and each particular kind has its own requirements as far as the preparations go.

Win/lose or win/win?

First of all, you have to determine whether you are about to enter what are commonly called win/lose negotiations or win/win negotiations, whether the emphasis of the negotiations will be on confrontation or on co-operation. In win/lose negotiations, parties strive for victory, they want to beat their opponent. In win/win negotiations they strive for consensus. They not only have no desire to beat their opponent but they want him to be satisfied with the outcome of the negotiations, too. In fact, they don't view him entirely as an opponent.

In win/lose negotiations each party tries to get as big a piece of the pie as possible (preferably he would like the entire pie) and to leave as little as possible for the opponent. In win/win situations, parties jointly try to make the pie larger before they start to divide it.

Some negotiators take the attitude that negotiating is by its very nature primarily a win/lose process. Others are convinced that all negotiations should be carried on in a win/win spirit. In my opinion neither of them is right. It all depends on the nature of the particular negotiations. Are you negotiating a long-term relationship? Is there a possibility that you will have to deal with the other party again in the future? Do you have to rely on him for loyal compliance with the agreement? Negotiate with a win/win attitude. Do not go for the last drop of blood. See to it that your opponent, too, is satisfied with the result. At the very least, leave his self-respect intact. Examples: joint-venture contracts, business partnerships, franchise agreements, fee arrangements between a lawyer and his client. In all these situations parties are not mere opponents. They intend to work together. They share many interests, although they have to discuss and solve some conflicting ones. It would harm the one if the other does not end up feeling good about the agreement.

But are you concerned with the well-being of the salesman from who you buy a second-hand car? No, all you want is the best car for the least money. And do you care in the least about the feelings of the loss adjuster of the insurance company of the brute who injured you in traffic? Not at all. The larger the settlement the better you feel and that's all you are interested in. One-off deals, short-term relationships, situations in which the other party cannot frustrate the implementation of the agreement lend themselves well to win/lose negotiating.

Keep two things in mind. First, win/win negotiating is a two-way business. You might prefer to negotiate in a win/win spirit, but if your opponent does not — even after you have tried to make him understand that he will gain by co-operation and lose by confrontation — you cannot afford to continue on the win/win road. You are largely forced to follow suit, whether you want to or not. However, if you are negotiating a relationship which in your opinion requires a mutual win/win approach, and if you notice that your opponent does not seem to think so, that in itself might prompt you to stop and wonder whether you should embark on a venture with that opponent at all. From the fact that you cannot negotiate with him in the way you think is suitable, you might deduce that you will not be able to do business with him later in the way you deem suitable. In that case you might seriously consider calling the whole thing off.

Another important, but often misunderstood, matter to remember is that the question whether or not you are sitting in the driver's seat at the negotiating table has no bearing on the decision whether to negotiate in a win/win or in a win/lose spirit. Even if your position is very strong, even if you could almost dictate your terms, it might be better for you in the long run not to abuse your power. Everything depends on the circumstances mentioned above, such factors as the duration of the relationship and how dependent you are on the other party for compliance. The only criterion continues to be how you view the negotiations in the context of the larger relationship.

Is agreement a must?

Ask yourself, as part of the preparations, whether the negotiations have to result in an agreement. Sometimes that's the case, often it's not. But in the heat of negotiation, negotiators frequently lose sight of the fact that not arriving at a deal is not the end of the world. They are so mesmerized by the excitement and challenge of the negotiations that emotionally they view non-agreement both as a disaster and a personal failure. The longer the negotiations drag on, the more prevalent this phenomenon becomes. And in those circumstances a nonsensical situation can develop, in which a negotiator is trying hard to obtain an outcome which will make him worse off than if no deal were struck at all.

A disagreement between two business partners, a strike, a marital dispute between a wife and husband who are not considering divorce, these are all situations which, some day, somehow, have to be resolved. Parties are stuck with each other. It is all but imperative that their negotiations result in an agreement. But negotiations about the purchase of a house, the hiring of an employee, the acquisition of a company, represent situations in which agreement might be very desirable but is not an absolute requirement. There are other houses which can be bought, other employees who can be hired and other companies which can be acquired. You only want the agreement if at the very least it's better than the status quo.

Generally there's a more acute necessity to arrive at a solution when problems arise in an existing relationship than when a new relationship is negotiated. In any case, determine before negotiations start whether or not, as far as you are concerned, the negotiations have to result in an agreement and keep in mind that in most instances, this is not the case.

Bilateral or multilateral negotiations?

Another aspect to concentrate on is whether more than two parties will be involved in the negotiations. Multilateral negotiations entail both the danger of and the opportunity for coalitions. Ask yourself whether it is probable that some of the other parties will join forces against you and what the implications of that would be. Also ask yourself whether it would make sense from your point of view to form a coalition with one or more other parties and, if so, decide how and when you're going to approach which party with which proposal.

Is the opponent internally divided?

Often the negotiation process consists of three areas of negotiation: one across the table, one within one party, one within the other. While preparing it's important to pay attention to these internal negotiations, both on your side and within the other party. Ask yourself whether your opponent might be internally divided and, if so, what the consequences will be; specifically, how you could capitalize on that.

A buyer dealing with a salesman of a large organization is often not only negotiating with that specific salesman, but through him with the sales manager, the credit manager, the legal department etc. All those people may be with the same company and look after the interests of that company but each one does it from his own vantage point. The salesman and the sales manager are primarily interested in making as many sales as possible. The credit manager only favours sales which do not entail undue credit risks. The legal department is concerned about the legalities. They are all on the same side, but they have different interests, different responsibilities, different points of view, different priorities, different degrees of willingness to take risks and to make concessions.

Will there be knock-on effects?

Another important question is whether the negotiations are somehow linked to future ones. Will precedents be set? Could anything you do, any decision you take, any concession you make, haunt you in the future? A company which deals with various unions knows that any concession it makes in negotiations with one union will be brought up in negotiations with another, sometimes to the extent that the latter union already takes the concession for granted. By the same token, is a union which deals with various companies constantly aware of the fact that every move it makes in negotiations might be used against it in negotiations with other companies? Granting discounts, pay rises and favours generally has knock-on effects. Pay attention to them when you prepare.

Is ratification required?

Ask yourself whether you and/or your opponent will have the final say or whether ratification, be it by members, a board of directors, a boss, a wife, a Parliament, to mention a few possibilities, will be required. As we shall see, this has a direct impact on the way negotiations have to be conducted. Always make sure at the start of negotiations whether or not your opponent has the final say. Nothing is more distressing and embarrassing than to hear from your opponent upon completion (at least that is what you were thinking) of the negotiations, something like 'very reasonable — all right as far as I'm concerned — I hope my boss will approve'.

7. Are the negotiations private or public?

There are pivotal differences between private and public negotiations, differences which you have to contemplate before the negotiations start. If a negotiator has to account publicly for what he is doing, for example to his members or to the media, that will have a direct impact on his behaviour at the negotiating table. Whatever he is doing or not doing, saying or not saying, he will not only be concerned about the effect on you, his opponent, but also about the effect on his audience. Show understanding of his position and grant him leeway to handle his 'public relations problem'.

Your opponent might, for example, tell you at the table that he finds a certain proposal which you are making very reasonable, but will portray that same proposal to his members as utterly unreasonable. Or, after a long, intense fight, he may reluctantly give in to one of your demands, which he has again and again called onerous and unreasonable, and later on, when criticized for having conceded, he may feel compelled to say that it was just a minor concession. And the other way around. If you make a concession which he disdainfully accepts as a minor, insignificant one, not deserving anything in return, he may in public describe that same concession as an important victory and proof of his negotiating acumen! Let him! Understand his position. Don't capitalize on the difficult situation he's in. Do not remind him of his inconsistencies. ('Now you say this, but yesterday on TV I heard you say that.')

In preparing for public negotiations you have to pay attention to the effects of the spotlight which is on you or your opponent. Will it help or hinder you? How can it benefit you? How can you minimize its negative effects? Should you at the start of the negotiations propose ground rules for dealing with the media? If so, what should they be?

8. Can the agreement be enforced?

One of the most important questions you have to ask yourself when you prepare for negotiations is whether compliance with the agreement which you hope to arrive at can be forced. I said it before and I will say it again: agreeing on a deal is one thing, getting the deal implemented is quite another. Sometimes an agreement is, either for practical or for legal reasons, unenforceable. Determining factors are the court system of the countries where parties are living, the solvency of your opponent, the nature of the deal (how can you force Nureyev to dance to the best of his ability; how can you force a researcher to come up with brilliant ideas?) and the nature of your relationship with your opponent (maybe you have the perfect right to sue somebody for non-compliance but if he is your best customer or if you cannot afford to have him as an enemy, that right can be entirely theoretical).

Whether or not compliance can be forced influences negotiations in all kinds of ways. In the days of the regime of Papa Doc Duvalier, I negotiated a joint venture with a government-controlled company in Haiti on behalf of a European company. Under the agreement my client would provide the capital and know-how and the Haitian company the natural resources. We were constantly aware that, if the agreement was not loyally executed by the Haitian company, my client would be virtually powerless. That added significantly to the risk which the company was assuming in this venture. It therefore attached the highest priority to getting back the funds invested as soon as possible and insisted on an initial division of profits. The Haitian company found this unreasonable and, from its vantage point, it was unreasonable. This is a good example of a situation where the substance of negotiations was directly shaped by the fact that compliance could not be forced.

Sometimes enforcement is possible but not a practical proposition. In Japan, for example, litigation is avoided whenever possible. That is one of reasons why the Japanese spend so much time getting to know each other, getting a feel for each other, at the start of negotiations. Although Japan has a first-class court system, the Japanese do not want to have to resort to it.

Will the other negotiator remain involved afterwards?

Sometimes the negotiators remain involved when it comes to implementation of the deal, sometimes they do not. In the first instance, you can assume that the spirit which has grown and possibly been carefully cultivated during the negotiations will continue in the implementation phase. If you have come to trust the opponent during the negotiations, you may assume that you can also trust him in the follow-up. You may find it unnecessary to discuss everything in detail, you may conclude that the spirit which dominated the negotiations will also dominate the implementation phase. But if you negotiate with an organization, you may very well never see Mr A, with whom you negotiated, again. And Mr B, Mr C and Mr D who are implementing the deal may be total strangers to you, very different in personality, mentality and reliability from Mr A and unaware of the spirit which prevailed at the negotiating table.

In general, when the negotiator will also be the implementer fewer i's have to be dotted and fewer t's have to be crossed.

10. Which parties are facing which deadlines?

Ask yourself while preparing whether your opponent, as far as you know, will be subject to any deadlines and, if so, which?

In negotiating, time is directly related to power. Time pressures and deadlines make negotiators vulnerable. Consider how you can capitalize on your opponent's deadlines.

Of course, pay attention to your own deadlines, too. Which ones do you have to cope with? How stringent are they? Can they be stretched? Is it likely that your opponent is aware of them?

11. Does your opponent really want an agreement?

Finally you must ask yourself whether your opponent really wants an agreement. It's not entirely uncommon for people to negotiate just for the sake of it (especially in politics; politicians often feel compelled by public opinion or other political considerations to go through the motions of negotiating without any desire to arrive at an agreement), for the sake of stalling (in the meantime trying to work out a deal with your competitor) or for the sake of gathering information/experience (no better way to get information from and about a competitor than to engage in merger negotiations with him).

If you cannot exclude the possibility that your opponent is not sincere, start off with a more reserved attitude, do not be too generous with information, ask more than you say and be alert for clues which either confirm or negate your suspicion.

13. The checklist for preparation

Once you have determined what kind of negotiations you are about to enter, the time has come for your checklist. Mine consists of the following items:

36

1 Fact-finding and/or review of past negotiations
2 Issues
3 Target — opening position — walk-away point
4 Best alternative
5 Arguments
6 Concessions
7 Inexpensive valuable concessions
8 Strengths and weaknesses
9 The opponent's vantage point
10 Strategy and tactics
11 Agenda
12 Dress rehearsal

Fact-finding

The first thing to do is to get as much information as possible about your opponent.

What is his financial situation?
Does he have internal problems?
What is his general reputation?
Does he live up to his commitments?
What is his reputation as a negotiator: Tough? A bluffer? Inclined to walk out?
What kind of decision-maker is he: Slow, cautious, inclined to rely on others? Or quick, impulsive, independent?
Is he subject to any time pressures? Which ones?
Why would he be interested in negotiating with you?
In other words: why does he want to make a deal?
And how eager will he be?
Who is the decision-maker (if you negotiate with a company)?

This kind of information helps you to get a feel for the strength of your bargaining position. If your opponent has financial problems, if time is working against him, if he is desperate to sell or buy, if he has no alternative but to deal with you, you may assume that the driver's seat will be yours. The information also helps you to decide how you're going to handle these specific negotiations, how you're going to approach your opponent, which tactics you're going to apply.

You may even find information which makes you wonder whether you want to deal with the opponent at all. His problems can be so overwhelming, his reputation so bad, his general behaviour so erratic, his word so worthless, that especially if you are going to negotiate a long-term relationship, you decide to break off the negotiations before even starting them.

How you get your information depends on the circumstances. If these are business negotiations, let's start with an obvious but often overlooked way: check with people within your own organization who dealt with him in the past. What's their opinion of the opponent? How do they remember the negotiations? And the follow-up? Go through the files on all the dealings which your company has had with the opponent in the more or less recent past. People within your opponent's organization (secretaries!) and his former employees are excellent sources. So are his bankers, competitors, customers and neighbours. Annual reports, local newspapers, trade magazines, court records, Dun & Bradstreet reports and your opponent's in-house magazine (if any) should be consulted. A credit check may reveal lots of useful information. Your solicitor and accountant could make some enquiries. But always refrain from spying and similar activities. They are not only unethical and often illegal, but they also almost always backfire. Ever heard of Watergate?

Keep one thing firmly in mind, however. Fact-finding sounds much more positive than it generally is. Often you do not find facts but what I call soft information, like opinions, assumptions, educated and not so educated guesses. When negotiating constantly make a mental distinction between hard facts and assumptions and continuously test and reassess the assumptions. You might have it from a good source that your opponent is in enviable financial shape, but if in the course of the negotiations you get an inkling that he may in fact have financial problems, do not reject that possibility, although it runs counter to your information. Somebody might have told you that your opponent is a mean so-and-so. Keep in mind that is just an opinion. Maybe he won't turn out to be so bad at all. Be aware of self-fulfilling prophecies. Often your expectations about how somebody will treat you determine the way you treat him. If your initial expectations are wrong, your attitude towards him will be wrong and you enter a vicious circle. Don't be intimidated if somebody has been described to you as an overpowering, masterful negotiator. Again, that's just an opinion, which may or may not be right.

So try to find as many facts as possible, but be prepared for the probability that you will end up with only a few facts and many questionable assumptions and opinions.

When you are about to negotiate abroad (or with people from another country) it is part of your fact-finding duties to educate yourself about that country, especially about its cultural and social values and customs which have a bearing on negotiating. I do not say 'when in Rome, do as the Romans do', but it is important to have some knowledge and some understanding of the people and the country.

When you have to negotiate in Japan, the last thing you should do is to try to imitate the Japanese style. But be aware that there is a Japanese negotiating style. Know that the Japanese way of doing business is quite different from the western one. Find out why that is the case and what the implications are. Don't be surprised when your Japanese counterpart spends, in your opinion, an inordinately long time on pleasantries and social chit-chat and never seems to get to business. He is not evasive or trying to stall, he just wants to know you better before he starts talking business with you. In fact, he sees you more as a future business partner than as an opponent and for a fruitful partnership it is essential to know each other quite well. Don't consider him cool and distant just because he does not call you by your first name. Every country has its own customs as far as the use of first names is concerned.

2. Review of past negotiations

Negotiations within an existing relationship or with an opponent whom you have known for a long time might not require much fact-finding. Instead, time should be spent on reviewing in your mind past negotiations with this opponent and evaluating how you fared in them. Did the negotiations go smoothly? Were you satisfied afterwards? If not, why not? What went wrong? Where does room for improvement lie? Do certain incidents stand out in your memory — mistakes on your part, amazing moves by your opponent? What can you learn from them? Which tactics is your opponent prone to use? How did you handle those tactics in the past? Has your opponent proved to be trustworthy? Does experience show that he implements in the same spirit as he negotiates? To what kind of concessions, arguments and behaviour does your opponent respond favourably? Where has he proved to be vulnerable? Which of his habits should you guard yourself against? Vivid and to the point reliving of past negotiations can be of tremendous help in preparing yourself for future ones.

3. The issues

Having gathered as much information as possible, you should list all the issues which have to be negotiated. Divide them into major and minor ones. That makes it easier for you while you're negotiating to realize whether you are discussing something of prime or lesser importance. In the heat of the moment, negotiators often lose sight of the relative importance of what is being discussed. They get so involved that they consider everything very important. It happens routinely that when, for example, ten hours are available for negotiating ten issues, negotiators almost unconsciously spend about one hour on each issue. But unequal issues do not deserve equal time.

Also ask yourself how the various issues interact. Can concessions on one issue be traded for concessions on others?

Look through the issues to the interests behind them. Are the issues to be discussed the real issues? Is the employee who wants to talk with you about a rise primarily concerned about better pay? Or does the rise essentially represent for him recognition, which could also be granted in another form: a larger room, broader duties, a more impressive title? Does the angry customer whom you're going to meet to discuss compensation for damages which he suffered because of a mistake you made really want money out of the discussion? Or are the real issues for him a better long-term relationship and guarantees that your mistakes will not be repeated? Not seldom the real issue behind the stated issue is merely a desire to receive an apology. However your opponent has framed the issue in such a situation, a mere apology will suffice to placate him.

4. Target — opening position — walk-away point

After having listed all the issues, you have to determine for each of them three basic positions: target, opening bid/offer and walk-away point.

Your target is what you are striving for. It should be as high as possible, without being unrealistic. What can you realistically expect if everything goes well for you? A negotiator should be ambitious, his targets should be high but he should not be a Don Quixote.

You get to your opening position by either adding to (seller) or subtracting from (buyer) your target position. How much varies from case to case. As a general rule, however, there should be quite some distance between your opening position and your target position, so that you will have enough room for manoeuvring and concession-making. But, extreme as it may be, the opening position should never be silly and always be defensible.

Your walk-away point (also called minimum settling point, or doorknob price) is your bottom line. It's very important to decide firmly before the negotiations start where you are going to draw the line. Protect yourself against the auction-trap. What happens if you go to an auction with your mind made up on what you are going to bid for but undecided on how much you are going to bid? If the price which you had in mind has been reached, you have the tendency to think that with one more bid the desired object will be yours (the triumph of hope over experience!). That one more bid easily becomes three or five more bids and the end result is that indeed you get what you wanted, but at a price which you might sorely regret.

In negotiating, as at auctions, you have to draw the line somewhere and you have to decide where to draw that line beforehand, when you are still objective, cool, unemotional, not tired, not influenced by excitement, by feelings of competing with or bidding against somebody else etc. Otherwise the same happens as at the auction. You think that with one more concession the deal will be done. But that one more concession will require a final concession and the final concession a final final concession. Before you know it, you have given away the store.

That does not mean that your 'WAP', your walk-away point, should be cast in concrete. Nothing in negotiating should be. Depending on the course of the negotiations, on the arguments used by your opponent, on the concessions he is willing to make on other issues etc, you may want or have to change your WAP but always consider it a drastic decision which has to be very well considered. I have the firm habit of never changing my WAP without calling for a break. Being away from the negotiating table, removed from the exciting atmosphere, I start to think as follows: 'I had good reasons to make such-and-such my WAP — when I took that decision I was cool, unemotional, objective, not tired — now I feel an urge to change my WAP — that by itself makes me suspicious — why do I have that urge? — is it a matter of convenience — is it the road of least resistance? — am I intimidated or over-impressed by my opponent? — or could it be that my reasons for being inclined to change the WAP are well founded? — what àre those reasons? — why do they justify and necessitate a change of my WAP?' And so on. Only if, after that mental process is completed, I'm still convinced that my WAP should be changed do I do so. But my decision on the second WAP has to be a very firm one again, not to be deviated from easily.

Sometimes negotiations will have to be entered with a few alternative WAPs for the same issue. If issues are interrelated, the WAP on one issue will depend on what can be obtained on the other issue. A buyer might draw the line at £70 if the price is all that is involved but might be willing to pay £71 if the seller gives him 60 days' credit and £72 if credit is extended to 90 days. A WAP will be different depending on who is going to bear the cost of shipping, handling and insurance. And somebody negotiating an employment contract will have to have various WAPs as far as the salary goes depending on the value of the remainder of the financial package, on the perks and on possible tax advantages. In those instances flexibility will be required. You cannot afford to have one fixed WAP for each separate issue. You will have to work with a combination of WAPs for all interrelated issues and you will have to be able to make on-the-spot shifts and trade-offs among all those WAPs. This requires above all else acute awareness of the cost of every concession you could make and the benefit to you of every concession the opponent is making.

5. Best alternative

The concept of a best alternative is of both psychological and strategic importance. You should always be aware of what the situation will be if no agreement is reached. What is your best alternative? Maybe you have hardly any alternative at all (businessman with liquidity problems negotiating with his bank about refinancing), maybe you have only an unattractive alternative, maybe your alternatives are not so bad at all and it might even be that you have excellent alternatives. Only if you know what your best alternative is are you really able to evaluate a proposed agreement. Everything is relative. No deal is good or bad in itself. It depends on what your alternatives are. Maybe you are not very enthusiastic about a certain deal, but if that deal exceeds your best alternative you should accept. Maybe a proposal is wonderful, but if your best alternative is even more wonderful, it should be rejected.

Your best alternative is the standard against which any proposed agreement should be measured. I have noted before that some negotiators are too emotionally committed to reaching an agreement, almost any agreement at all. They forget about their alternatives. Not reaching an agreement is regarded as a failure. Of course, only agreements which are better than the available alternatives should be considered.

Spend time on developing your best alternative. It has a direct impact on the power relationship between you and your opponent. The relative power of negotiating parties depends on how (un)attractive to each one the option of not reaching agreement is. If you know that you have a viable alternative in case no agreement is reached, you feel better, you have more power. In fact, if you have an attractive alternative it often makes sense to let your opponent know about it. A good alternative means less dependency on your part and therefore more pressure on your opponent. On the other hand, be sceptical if your opponent suggests that he has perfect alternatives. One of the most common forms of deception in the negotiating process is to say, suggest or imply that you don't need your opponent at all, that you have many alternatives, that your only real problem is an abundance of choices.

Arguments

Take stock of all your arguments in support of each position you are going to take. Try to anticipate your opponent's counter-arguments. Prepare your rebuttal of these counter-arguments. Discuss every issue in your mind, taking the parts of both yourself and your opponent.

Concessions

For each issue decide which concessions you're prepared to make in which stage of the game and in which order. Also verify how much each of them costs. Often negotiators do not have the faintest idea about the cost, especially the long-term cost, of their concessions.

Inexpensive valuable concessions

As we have seen, a negotiator should be creative and inventive. One way to make use of these talents is to think up concessions which cost you little but which have great value for the opponent. That is *the* way to make the pie larger before dividing it. What better way to make both parties happy than for them to give a lot to but take just a little from each other? If you use a credit card the merchant has to pay a small percentage of the purchase price to the credit card company. As far as the price goes, using or not using your credit card does not make any difference to you. But it does make a difference to the merchant. So it's easier for him to give you a discount, in essence a free concession if you pay him cash instead of using your credit card.

Quite often the tax implications of a transaction provide opportunities for this kind of concession. Part of a purchase price may be shaped as a deductible donation. In an international transaction it may be that only one party can make use of the tax benefits. Nothing makes better sense than shifting all the tax benefits to that party in return for a better deal for the other party. And to give a very different example: if you buy a house from a building contractor, you might be able to afford to raise the price somewhat if he undertakes to perform some conversion work which you would want to do anyway. It would cost him much less than it would cost you if you had the work done by an outsider.

So concentrate on what goodies you can offer your opponent which are relatively cheap to you. And also vice versa. What has little value for him but could be important for you?

Strengths and weaknesses

Not all your points, positions and arguments will be equally strong and reasonable. Determine objectively where you're strong and where you're weak. Decide how you're going to capitalize on your strengths and how you're going to cover up your weaknesses.

The opponent's vantage point

Preparing entails avoiding surprises to the greatest possible extent. Put yourself into your opponent's shoes. Which issues will be the major and minor ones for him? Which will be his targets? How is he going to open? What will be his bottom line? What alternatives does he have? What arguments would you use if you had to argue his position? Which concessions can you expect from him? What are his strengths and weaknesses?

Of course, all this is primarily guesswork, but often it's a matter of educated guesses. The more experienced you are, but above all the more you force yourself to look at the situation through his eyes, the more reliable your guesses will turn out to be.

10. Strategy and tactics

Matters of strategy and tactics have to be considered in advance of the negotiations themselves. What will your strategy be? What are your overall goals? Which tactics are you going to apply? In which vein are you going to negotiate? Friendly, co-operative, flexible? Or does it serve a purpose to take a tough, cool, rigid attitude? Is it to your advantage to rush the negotiation or should you take it easy? Are you going to insist on long sessions and intervals or do you opt for short ones? Very important: what authority do you have or, more broadly, do you want to have? As we shall see, it can be good tactics to negotiate with limited authority. If your opponent has limited authority it is almost always best not to have the final say yourself. What are the limits of your mandate? How are you going to use them? How are you going to explain them to your opponent?

If you negotiate with a team, you have to decide on a role for each team member. Somebody has to be in charge. Someone, not necessarily the same person, has to be the spokesman. Somebody else could be primarily the observer, the note-taker. In any case, before the negotiations start it should be clear to each member of the team what will be expected of him.

You might also reflect on quasi-issues, demands which you make just for the sake of enabling you to concede them — at a price. I once had to hire somebody for a specific project. I found the ideal candidate, but it was essential for me that he would start on 1 July. That would be impossible, he told me. He absolutely could not start before 1 October. The fact that he said so only after I had stressed the importance of 1 July should have made me suspicious. Anyway, after a lot of pressure from me, he finally made the grand gesture (suggesting that it was a huge sacrifice for him) of making himself available as from 1 July. But not before I had bettered the terms of his employment considerably.

Negotiating involves making concessions. We have seen that concessions which cost you little but which are of great value to the opponent are good ones. But the perfect ones are those concessions which don't cost you anything at all!

11. Agenda

You are now at the point where you must decide on the agenda, more precisely on your proposal for an agenda, because your opponent has still to agree it. In fact, agendas themselves are often the subject of negotiations. It may be to the tactical advantage of one party to discuss certain issues in a certain sequence. That in itself may be a reason for the other party to insist on another sequence.

Often the agenda cannot be detailed before proposals and counter-proposals have been spelled out. It may be only at the negotiating table that you find out what the issues are for your opponent. But at a certain moment there has to be an agenda which is complete and specific as to the issues which have to be discussed. Although there are exceptions to this rule, no new issues should be brought up in the course of the negotiations and no new demands should be made which go beyond the agenda.

Generally it's best to start with the easier issues. Solving them creates a co-operative atmosphere which facilitates the solution of the more thorny issues. Moreover, the more issues there are that have been solved and the more time the parties have invested fruitfully, the more they feel committed to bringing the entire negotiations to a successful end. There is almost a domino effect. Solving one issue enhances the odds for a solution of the next issue.

As always, this is only a general rule. Sometimes it is better to reverse the sequence. In collective labour contract negotiations, for example, the employer might prefer to start with the sticky issues. If they have been solved, it is unlikely that the union will call a strike over minor issues even if they cannot be solved easily. As soon as the major issues have been settled, the union has in effect lost its strike weapon.

There is a third alternative. Especially in situations where an agreement is a must (so that it is unlikely that an early impasse about a hard issue will bring the entire negotiations to an untimely end), I sometimes strive deliberately for a mix of hard and easy issues in order to provide parties with some breathing space between fights. After the solution of a hard issue the negotiators can, as it were, cool off and relax while discussing a few easy ones.

Deadlines should be a factor in drawing up the agenda. When your opponent will have to cope with a deadline, it makes sense to postpone issues which are important for you, and also issues regarding which your arguments are not very strong, for later in the game. Then the imminent deadline might make your opponent easier to deal with. By the same token, if you yourself face a deadline you should see to it that issues which are important for you are discussed at an early stage.

These observations about the agenda apply to negotiations in which the issues are separated, in which parties try to reach agreement on one issue before moving on to the next. These are negotiations in which the final agreement consists of the sum of the settlements of all the individual issues. That is not always the case. In Japan, for example, issues are not split up. They are reviewed and discussed in increasing detail, and agreement is *only* reached on the entire package.

Incidentally, this is another example of why it is important to be aware of the negotiating style of your counterpart. When a westerner who is uninformed in this respect negotiates in Japan it can happen that, after the discussions have been going on for a long time with no agreement on even one of the issues, he gets the feeling that no headway is being made. In order to get things moving, he starts to make concessions. Unnecessarily, because as far as his Japanese counterpart is concerned, they are not yet at the stage of requiring and making concessions.

12. Dress rehearsal

The final item on your checklist is admittedly a luxury item, in the sense that you will often not have the time for it. It is very helpful, however, if shortly before the negotiations start, you could have a dry run within your organization or with a colleague or friend.

Let a colleague play your opponent, as realistically as possible, and negotiate with him. Even better, play the opponent yourself, be the devil's advocate. However, there can be a danger in that. I once negotiated with somebody who told me afterwards that for the first few hours of the negotiation he was confused because the day before he had been playing me with such conviction and success that he found it difficult to revert to being himself again.

Once I was retained by a client who was considering the purchase of a certain kind of company. He had checked the market and had decided that he would like to acquire company A or company B or company C in that order of preference. He would love to have A, like to own B and would be wholly satisfied with C. He wanted me to negotiate the acquisition. He gave me a large budget so that I didn't have to be too cost-conscious and there was no rush. The first decision I had to make was with whom I would start to negotiate. With A, B or C? Or maybe with all three of them at the same time, not in the sense that I would meet them at the same time in the same room at the same negotiating table, but in the sense that, for example, I would start to talk with A on Monday morning, schedule a meeting with B for Monday afternoon and one with C for Tuesday morning, and so on.

Either choice had its pros and cons and could be defended, but I decided to start negotiating with C. Why? Because by doing so I would learn a lot which I could use in my subsequent dealings with B and, having progressed ever further on the learning curve by negotiating with B, I would be perfectly prepared for talking to A, my client's first choice. The negotiations with B and C were almost real-life dry runs.

Of course, I did not negotiate with B and C to the extent that I arrived at a deal with them. When a deal came close, I discontinued or slowed down the negotiations in order to embark on negotiations with the other parties. And I never intimated to B and C that I was talking only to them. Doing so would have been unethical and, moreover, it was to my client's advantage that they knew that he had alternatives. Talking about ethics, I stress that both B and C were serious candidates. I was not abusing them just for the sake of the learning process.

I mention this experience as an example of preparing by doing. But there was another advantage in handling the situation this way. By negotiating with C, I gained a rather good idea of what kind of agreement could be worked out with that company. That agreement, which appeared to be within reach, served as a floor for my subsequent negotiations. When I ultimately negotiated with A, I had a sound idea of what my client could get from B and C. In other words, I knew what his fall-back position, his best alternative was. And that considerably strengthened my bargaining position in relation to A.

When you use this checklist you can be sure that, normally speaking, all important items have been considered. But in specific negotiations specific items might have to be added to your personal negotiating checklist. And if the negotiations take place in more than one round, you have to go through the checklist again in advance of each successive round, updating and refining all the decisions which you made when you started to prepare, in view of everything which has happened or been learned in the meantime.

Chapter 4

Aspirations and Concessions

Aspirations

Your aspiration level consists of your goals, your expectations and the standards you set for yourself. It is a well-known fact that the higher you aim, the more you achieve. Ample research has also demonstrated that the outcome of negotiations tends to be rather close to the targets of experienced negotiators, provided these targets have been set realistically.

An exercise at my negotiating seminars supports this finding. We simulate negotiations between the victim of an air crash and the loss adjuster of the airline's insurance company, about compensation for damages. The participants are split up into three groups and each group into pairs of negotiators (the victim and the adjuster). Everybody gets a brief description of the case, which is exactly the same for everyone except in one respect. In the first group, the instructions for both the adjuster and the victim say that cases like this are generally settled for £500,000. In the second group, both the victim and the adjuster are told that these cases are generally settled in the neighbourhood of £125,000. The victim in the third group gets as a confidential piece of information that similar cases are often settled at about £500,000 while the adjuster is told that such cases are generally settled in the neighbourhood of £125,000. And what invariably happens? The negotiators in the first group settle at around £500,000, the negotiators in the second group at around £125,000 and the negotiators in the third group deadlock. The parties who succeed in working out an agreement settle at around their aspiration level. The parties who negotiate with very different aspiration levels are bound to fail.

If aspiration levels have such a direct impact on the outcome of negotiations, it follows that it is very important to influence the aspiration level of your opponent downwards. The lower his aspiration level is and the more dents it has suffered, the better the outcome of the negotiations is likely to be for you.

Aspiration levels can be moved up and down. Success raises them, failure brings them down. There are two other laws applying to aspiration levels: the longer negotiations take, the more they tend to erode; and they erode more quickly when somebody negotiates alone than when he negotiates as a member of a team.

All this has some important practical consequences. The first is that 'do the best you can' is a bad mandate. It provides no clear target, no stimulating aspiration level for the negotiator. He is not committed to any kind of outcome. His aspiration level is very vulnerable.

A second consequence is that if you force yourself not to be too optimistic, not to expect too much in order to avoid disappointment later, you make yourself the victim of a self-fulfilling prophecy. By consciously lowering your aspiration level, you become a less effective negotiator.

A third and very important implication is that give-away concessions, goodwill concessions, in other words easy successes for the opponent, tend to raise his aspiration level. Instead of softening him up, as you intended to do, they make him greedy for more concessions. Instead of reducing the size of the difference between you, they magnify it. Instead of promoting settlement, they will impede it.

And a last consequence of practical importance is that sometimes extreme initial demands or offers, provided they are not absurd and can be supported rationally, are very effective because they cause a fatal blow to the aspiration level of the opponent. Shock him with your opening offer! That will compel him to reconsider his expectations. It may even make him change his opening position (his asking price, his first offer) before he has had the chance to mention it.

What seller of a car who has an asking price of £10,000 in mind still dares to ask that price after a serious buyer opens the bidding with £4,000? Often it is good tactics from the buyer's point of view to praise the object first before making the shockingly low offer. If a buyer walks in and starts to criticize the car in each and every respect, the seller is entirely prepared for a low offer. That offer will hardly affect him and certainly not make him change his asking price right away. But if a buyer comes in praising the car, mentioning that he can see right away that the car has always been cared for, referring to the low mileage, paying a compliment about the new tyres, informing the seller that he has been looking for such a car for a long time, if such an apparently knowledgeable and reasonable buyer makes an offer, it's hard just to shrug that offer off. The buyer has created legitimacy for his offer. While he was praising the car, the seller's aspiration level went up quickly, but collapsed as soon as he made his offer. The seller starts to wonder whether his price is realistic, reasonable and attainable. The chances are that he will not counter the £4,000 bid with the £10,000 he had decided on before the buyer walked in, but with a much lower asking price. *Unless he has all the time in the world i.e. is Agreement paramount?*

Shockingly low offers have other positive spin-offs. They provide ample room for making concessions. Furthermore, everything being relative, subsequent offers will look good compared to the shockingly bad first offer. And by making a very low (but, I repeat, not absurd) offer, a negotiator communicates firmness, resolve, experience. He suggests that he is not to be trifled with.

But only take an extreme opening position if you are prepared to stick to it, or in its region, for some time. If it is followed by quick, easy, large concessions, an extreme initial offer becomes counter-productive and, after the initial dent, the opponent's aspiration level is raised considerably.

Knowing that you can reduce your opponent's aspiration level and even his opening position with a shockingly low offer, you should brace yourself for the possibility that your opponent will try to do the same to you. Never let your initial demand be influenced by your opponent's opening offer. Stick to the one you had decided on, presumably for good reasons, during your preparations. Do not let your opponent's extreme opening position set the tone for the negotiations.

These reflections on aspiration levels should put an end to the usual misconceptions about concessions. It's not necessarily true that they are useful to get negotiations on their way, that they create goodwill, that they will make opponents reciprocate. They may suggest weakness and make opponents smell surrender. They may irreparably harm the credibility of the negotiator who retreats from a firmly taken position. When they are made too easily and quickly, they tend to make opponents suspicious. Why would a concession be made so quickly and easily? Too good to be true! What's the catch?

Of course, negotiators have to make concessions all the time. But they should know what they are doing and realize that certain concessions are called for in certain situations, while the same concessions will be counter-productive in others. Making concessions is often the road of least resistance, the easy thing to do. Concessions can be necessary, positive and helpful, but they can also be detrimental to the cause of reaching agreement.

Do NOT give anything away you do NOT have to. Give Freebies

51

The do's and don'ts of concession-making

So the first rule in the area of concession-making is that you always have to consider whether the situation and the context are right for the specific concession you have in mind. Realize that concessions are not by and in themselves positive moves, that they can become obstacles to a solution.

The second rule should be never to accept a first offer. Hardly ever is the first offer also the final offer. First offers are made on the assumption that concessions will be required. In fact, if you accept his first offer you often frustrate your opponent. He will assume that his first offer was much better than required and he will feel foolish for making an unnecessarily generous offer.

How about the following situation? Somebody wants to sell his house. He's about to put an ad in the newspaper with an asking price of £100,000. Out of the blue, somebody comes along and offers him £100,000. Should the seller summarily accept? Should he proceed with his plan to advertise and ask the buyer to come back in a few weeks? Should he reject the £100,000 offer and negotiate for more?

When I submit this question at my negotiating seminars, it always leads to a lively discussion. Some people prefer to accept without any haggling. Why be greedy? Why not be glad that, without any trouble and costs, you get your price? From a philosophical point of view they may be right, but from a negotiator's point of view are not. As a negotiator you should never accept a first offer. The odds are overwhelmingly that the buyer is prepared to offer more, that he offered £100,000 on the assumption that at some point he would have to raise his offer. His offer might also indicate that the asking price was too low. Moreover, the seller hardly runs any risk by trying to get more. In the exceptional case that the buyer's first offer would also prove to be his final offer, there's no reason why the seller could not still accept the £100,000 offer.

Proceeding with the plan to advertise is dangerous. The buyer might find another house in the meantime. Moreover, if the seller appears at his door two weeks later, suddenly willing to discuss a sale, the buyer will conclude, and rightly, that the ad has not resulted in a flood of offers.

The third alternative, negotiating for more, is as we have seen, the right one for the negotiator. Most probably he will be able to raise the price. Moreover, the buyer will be much more satisfied if he has to negotiate about the price.

Let's go over a few other do's and don'ts which apply to concession-making.

Always give yourself room to negotiate and to make concessions. In other words, start high (seller) or low (buyer). If your opening and your target positions are too close to each other you are either forced to take a very rigid negotiating attitude or you will have to water down your targets.

See to it that your opponent will be the first to make a concession, especially on major issues. You might consider conceding relatively insubstantial issues at the beginning in order to extract counter-concessions later on more critical items, but let your opponent be the first to budge on major issues. The value of concessions grows over time, so conserve your concessions as long as possible. The longer your opponent has to wait for them, the harder he has to fight for them, the more valuable they become and the more he will appreciate them.

If you make concessions, make them small and make them slowly. Smaller and more slowly than your opponent does. But try to hide how tight-fisted you are being. It is easier said than done, but if you can impart an impression of flexibility while in fact you're hardly retreating from your position, you have the best of two worlds.

In the area of concessions there should be no quid pro quos. The fact that your opponent makes a concession does not mean that you have to make one in return. And what is a concession? If you offer £100,000 for a house which has about that value and your opponent asks £150,000, should the fact that he reduces his asking price to £140,000 be viewed and treated as a concession? No, not at all. Your reaction should be that his entirely untenable position has only become just a little bit less untenable. In my book, a real concession is only made when a negotiator retreats from his realistic targets, not when he does so from an unrealistic position.

Try to get something in return for every concession you make. If not, your opponent will start to expect free concessions. And if your opponent makes free concessions, well, that's his privilege but it should not be any reason for you to reciprocate.

One way to avoid making free concessions is to put a string on your concessions. Make contingent concessions, if-concessions. 'If I were willing to do this and this, would you then concede on that and that?' The advantages of such contingent concessions are twofold. You do not give anything away for free and, moreover, you find out what your opponent's reaction to a potential concession will be before you make it. You can still keep the status quo if you find that the concession would not have the desired effect.

We have noted already that concessions which cost you little or nothing but are valuable to your opponent (or vice versa) play a very constructive role in negotiations. But if you make such a concession, even though it costs you little or nothing, make a big deal out of it. Your concession is worthwhile to your opponent, so why let him know that it was hardly a sacrifice? By the same token, be cautious in identifying which of your demands and wishes are important to you. Otherwise you give your opponent the opportunity to make a lot of fuss about the fact that he's meeting those demands, even if doing so does not mean a thing to him.

I once participated on behalf of an American company in collective labour contract negotiations on a small island in the Caribbean. The company and the union were on very bad terms at the time. Moreover, the tensions between the company and the union had become a social and political issue on the island. The negotiations had reached dimensions which went beyond the interests of the parties themselves. In that charged atmosphere, the president of the company held a press conference on his arrival at the airport, in which he made an unfortunate remark which could be construed as having racial overtones.

When we met to prepare for the negotiations, the president was the first to admit that his comments had been stupid and improper and that apologies were in order. It was decided that he would make those apologies at the very start of the negotiations. However, when we walked into the negotiating room the next day he did not even get the chance to apologise. The union officials were all over him, screaming at him, insulting him, demanding apologies. They refused to discuss anything else except their demand for apologies. That made us change gear. Instead of doing what we had decided to do, offer apologies, we resisted the union's demand. For days the negotiations were entirely limited to a discussion about the apologies. When we finally agreed to make them, the union was gladly willing to make, in return for what they considered to be a huge sacrifice on our part, important concessions on what we considered to be, and what in fact were, the real issues.

In previous chapters, a few rules about concessions were mentioned which bear repetition. Obtain concessions by creating problems for your opponent which you can solve – at a price. Demand something which is of little value for you, but important to him, in order to enable yourself to drop that demand in exchange for a real concession on his part. Always be aware of what a concession you're considering will cost you, especially in the long run. Seemingly minor concessions in a long-term contract can add up to a fortune. Right until final agreement you can take back concessions which you made. You should consider doing so if you are dealing with an opponent who cannot be convinced that your bottom line really has been reached. Make it clear to him that he should accept on the spot, before your offer erodes further.

Be alert for the possibility that your opponent would like to retreat from a position previously taken, but does not know how to do it without losing face or credibility. Make it easy for him to yield. Give him the feeling that he's hardly making a concession and that, in any case, he's not losing face or credibility at all.

Keep a tally of your concessions and those of your opponent. It's useful to keep a check on yourself. Are you making too many, too valuable concessions too fast? You can also use that list to show your opponent that so far the negotiations have been a one-way street and that it's his turn now for a few concessions. Make a mental distinction between real concessions (concessions by which you retreat from a realistic target) and quasi-concessions (concessions by which you simply come back from a position which you took fully aware that you would not be able to stick to it).

One of the most simplistic concepts in negotiating is splitting the difference. It sounds fair but whether it is depends entirely on what the positions are at the time when the splitting is being suggested. Splitting the difference between a reasonable and an unreasonable position results in an unreasonable outcome. If somebody suggests that you split the difference, proceed as if he has already conceded half the difference. If the seller of a house proposes to split the difference between his asking price of £120,000 and your last offer of £100,000, proceed as if the seller has already lowered the price to £110,000 and try to negotiate that amount down.

By the same token, if your opponent offers a price 'somewhere between £1000 and £2000' or a price of '£300 to £400', or a price 'in the £600 area', translate those prices in your mind as £2000, £400 and, for example, £800. Demands and offers should be phrased in specific numbers. If not, the opponent will start at the end of the range which is best for him, and proceed from there.

When the negotiations are completed, never tell your opponent that he made more concessions than necessary and that he got fewer concessions than you were prepared to make. Don't rub it in! In essence you are telling him that he is an inept negotiator. He will remember that in the implementation phase or when you meet him at the negotiating table next time.

Moreover, renegotiating an agreement is not that unusual. If your opponent knows that you would have been satisfied with a lesser agreement, he will be inclined to find reasons or pretexts to make you renegotiate. And he will come to the renegotiating-table with lots of crucial information, provided by your own good self!

Finally: different concession patterns send different messages. It not only matters how large your concessions are, but also in what manner and sequence you make them. Let's assume for illustration's sake that you are prepared to reduce your initial demand by £80,000 and that there will be four negotiating rounds. All kind of concession patterns are possible.

You could, for example, stick to your initial demand throughout the first three rounds and make an £80,000 concession in the fourth round. In the first three rounds you appear very firm, you almost give the impression that your first offer will also be your final offer. The result could be that your opponent gives up before the negotiations ever get to a fourth round and that you will get away without making any concession at all. But if not, the negotiations will take a dramatic turn. Suddenly you make a huge concession, which will greatly boost your opponent's expectations and aspiration level. It will be hard for you to convince him that that large concession will be the only one you're prepared to make.

You could also make four concessions of £20,000 each. Such a concession pattern does not put any pressure on your opponent. It will make him expect similar concessions in each round. It would be even worse if you were to increase your concessions gradually. Let's say you start with a concession of £10,000 and follow up with a £15,000 concession. If that one does not suffice, you make a £25,000 concession, which you follow up with a £30,000 concession. If there is one way to make negotiations drag on forever, this is it. Your opponent will conclude that the longer the negotiations continue, the better the deal will become for him. His aspiration level is constantly on the rise.

But take a look at the same concessions in the reverse order, from £30,000, via £25,000 and £15,000 to £10,000. When you make concessions in this sequence, you show abundant but also decreasing willingness to compromise. Your opponent will infer that further concessions are unlikely.

You could also make your concessions like this: first round £59,000, second round £20,000, third round nothing, fourth round £1,000. The drawback of this approach is that the first concession might be unnecessarily generous and unduly raise your opponent's aspiration level. Thereafter, however, he will be quickly discouraged and conclude that your willingness to make concessions really has dried up. A variant would be to start with a £60,000 concession, followed by a £20,000 concession. Then you take £10,000 back to signal that if your opponent continues to haggle the deal will only get worse for him. In the fourth round, assuming that he got the message and that he is willing to conclude the deal, you could restore the £10,000 concession, as a way to force him over the threshold.

It cannot be stated in general what is the right and what the wrong pattern for making concessions. Everything depends on the circumstances – although I cannot think of any instance in which increasing your concessions continuously and predictably would be advisable. The only point I have tried to make is that, when you have determined that concessions are called for, you should also pay attention to the manner, sequence and pattern in which you are going to make them.

Deadlocks

Many deadlocks exist only in the eye of the beholder! Let's assume you are selling your house. Your target is £100,000, your asking price £120,000 and your absolute minimum £90,000. After some haggling, the buyer offers £96,000. You are convinced that by holding out somewhat longer you can obtain a better offer. So you reject the £96,000 and insist on more, let's say £105,000. Both you and the buyer stick to your positions. The buyer thinks there is a deadlock. The £9,000 gap appears too large to be bridged. But you know for a fact that there will be a deal. The offer which you have in hand already exceeds your absolute minimum considerably and, if it cannot be bettered, you will accept it. So there only *seems* to be a deadlock. And solely to the buyer.

Apart from deadlocks which are no deadlocks, there are deadlocks which one of the parties has created almost on purpose. Brinkmanship can be an effective means to show your determination, strength and resolve and to test those of the opponent. Bring him to the edge of an impasse and see how he reacts. Does he remain firm? Does he still talk big? Does he still manage to radiate self-confidence? Often negotiators change remarkably when a deadlock comes close. And the fact that you do not seem to be afraid of a deadlock seldom goes unnoticed.

Of course, brinkmanship can be risky. You never know exactly how far you can go, where you cross the brink. So you take the risk that a deadlock will indeed develop. But generally that risk is not so grave. If you have deliberately taken the risk of a deadlock, it is almost always possible to break the impasse. Returning to the table with the message that you have thought things over, that you have discussed the situation within your organization, that you have some new suggestions, that you have thought up some alternatives, will more often than not suffice to get the discussion going again. You might have lost some face and credibility but that is part of the game.

It is my experience that in large organizations deadlocks are often more frowned upon than bad settlements. As a result, their negotiators tend to be over-wary of deadlocks. And the longer the negotiations take and the further people have travelled for the negotiations (and, I might add; the more exotic and sunny the negotiating location is) the more this holds true. A friend of mine, living in a chilly country in Europe, negotiated for two weeks in Hawaii. He worked very hard but in vain. No agreement was reached. So he came back with empty hands but with a perfect tan, looking well rested, in great shape. Nobody had any doubt how he had been spending his time. Surfing, sunbathing, swimming, everything except negotiating! Needless to say, if you are on the other side, you can and should capitalize on the fact that for negotiators of larger organizations it is often easier to come back with a disappointing settlement than with no agreement at all.

I have said that some deadlocks only seem to be deadlocks and that others can easily be solved. Sometimes, however, a real and nasty deadlock develops. There is a tough problem. Both parties want to solve it, but they are too far apart. The negotiations are stuck and, in spite of the sincere efforts of both parties, remain stuck. What can be done to break such a real deadlock?

Means to break an impasse

If the deadlocking issue is one out of a larger agenda, set that issue temporarily aside. Agree to disagree on it for the time being. Move the discussion on to issues which have not yet proved controversial. Solving those issues will improve the climate, engender optimism, show that agreement is possible. Moreover, if a deal has been completed for 90 per cent of the agenda, the incentive to take the last hurdle, too, is great. Suddenly the deadlocking issue might not seem so unmanageable any more.

Taking a break can perform miracles. Often an impasse arises because of fatigue and loss of creativity, because negotiators are seeing too much of each other, parties are running around in circles. Everything might seem different when they meet again after a few days.

A milder and often useful way to break off the negotiations temporarily is to leave the negotiating table but to continue informal discussions in a different atmosphere, on a golf course, in a restaurant or, in Scandinavian countries, a sauna.

Involving higher-ups may help. Generally they have not been affected by a deteriorating bargaining atmosphere. They can look at the problems from another angle in a broader context. They have more authority to take decisions which can break the impasse. Making concessions is often easier for them.

In negotiations between teams it often helps to replace one or more negotiators. Impasses can be due to bad chemistry between negotiators. If only two negotiators are involved and both of them are replaced, a very positive phenomenon tends to occur. Competition starts between the old negotiators and the new ones. The new ones, although they are at different ends of the table, have a common purpose; to show that they can do better than their predecessors. They feel their joint duty is to achieve what their predecessors could not: to bring about an agreement.

If it is absolutely clear that the parties themselves cannot solve the impasse, it's possible to call in a mediator. They frequently succeed in their mission. One reason for their success rate is probably the fact that if the parties can agree on the appointment of a mediator, they are still very much on speaking terms and motivated to arrive at an agreement. But there is an aspect of self-fulfilling prophecy which comes into play. In situations where parties expect a mediator to be involved at some stage, they often have the tendency to save something for him. They withhold a concession or two because they know that in practice a mediator will require further concessions from both sides. It may be that if parties had not held back a little in anticipation of the mediator, they would not have needed a mediator at all!

The last way to break a deadlock is one which can only be used in special circumstances. But in those circumstances it can be very effective. It's called 'last offer, best offer'. It's worth trying when the gap between the positions of both parties is not as large as all that and both parties really want to bridge that gap. It works as follows. A third person is appointed. This person may try to solve the problem by mediation. If that does not work, both parties have to put their very last offer on paper and it is in their own interest to make that very last offer as reasonable, as fair — as conciliatory if you will — as possible, because the third person has to choose between the two proposals and whichever he chooses becomes the agreement. He may not change anything in any proposal. It is either A or B, and because the third person can be expected to choose the proposal which he deems the most reasonable and fair, both parties are under great pressure to really put pressure on themselves in formulating their final proposal.

The situation they're in is comparable to the cutting or choosing dilemma. It might seem nice that you may cut the cake but, if you do not divide it into two absolutely equal parts, the other party will take the larger. So the only way to help yourself, at least not to hurt yourself, is to be entirely fair and honest.

'Last offer, best offer' worked well when a client of mine was trying to negotiate a merger. The negotiations went so well that after a while both parties were convinced that an agreement would be reached. In anticipation of the merger, they started to operate largely as one company, although the negotiations were not yet concluded. Suddenly some problems came up which could not be resolved, although everybody tried their very best. The differences were important, but not irreconcilable. Both parties were eager to agree. Practically speaking, there was not even a way back for them any more. 'Last offer, best offer' brought a solution which everybody was satisfied with.

Chapter 6

The Role of Time

Time plays an important and often decisive role in negotiations.

For negotiators, time is power. When you are in a rush (whether it is because you urgently need a result, you have other meetings planned, you have lots of work waiting for you, you have a plane to catch, you are about to leave on holiday or for whatever reason) you are at a distinct disadvantage. Try to avoid negotiating in these circumstances. And at least try to keep your opponent unaware of your time problem.

Time pressures inevitably make negotiators lower their targets, water down their demands and increase their concessions. Worse than that: they themselves are often not aware of what they're doing.

Take your time! Both for the negotiations themselves and for proper preparation of them. Not taking time for either is the first concession you are making to your opponent. A crucial and unnecessary one, given for free!

Don't assume too easily that you don't have the time. Time is almost always a matter of priorities. Do you really lack time? In other words, did you, after thoughtful consideration, rationally decide that other matters should have a higher priority? Or do you not have time because you are underestimating the importance of being well prepared? Do you understand what the difference in outcome between a well negotiated and quick deal could be? Do you realize how much money you are losing by lowering your demands and increasing your concessions because of time pressures? Doing so when you are negotiating a long-term contract may cost you a fortune over the longer term.

Taking your time for negotiating also has a psychological impact. You exude an air of being cool, relaxed, unhurried and unharried, in command of the situation. There is a lesson in the negotiations almost 20 years ago in Paris between North Vietnam and the USA. Simply by taking a lease on a house for two years, the North Vietnamese gave a very clear-cut message to the Americans (who were staying on a daily basis in expensive hotels): they were not in a rush, they had all the time in the world, in spite of all the horrors of the continuing war they would negotiate unencumbered by time pressures. Time would not force them to accept anything which they would not consider acceptable.

Rush deals

Even to the 'thou shall not negotiate in a hurry' commandment there are exceptions. In my experience quick negotiations tend to result in extreme deals, very good for one side, very bad for the other. Moreover, in quick negotiations, skilled negotiators invariably prevail over unskilled counterparts and well-prepared ones over their ill-prepared opponents. Therefore it makes sense to rush negotiations if you have good reasons to believe that you are more skilled and better prepared than your opponent. You might take him by surprise and end up with a very good deal. But such a surprise attack should only be considered in win/lose situations. In win/win negotiations you want to avoid at all cost leaving your opponent with the feeling that he has been bulldozed. Furthermore, especially in win/win situations, the quality of the agreement should receive attention. A lopsided agreement is rarely of high quality.

Deadlines

What if you are entirely willing to make enough time available for negotiations but you are faced with a deadline? First, deadlines are often self-inflicted. Time is running out on you because you started too late. Second, make a distinction between objective deadlines and arbitrary ones. Objective deadlines are the result of circumstances which cannot be altered. Examples are court dates and expiration dates of a contract. If law suits are to be settled out of court it has to be before the court decides. A collective labour contract has to be negotiated before the old one expires. Although these deadlines are not totally rigid (the other party in the law suit might consent to a postponement, parties in collective labour contract negotiations can agree to extend the existing contract temporarily while negotiating a new one), they are determined by the circumstances, not by the parties involved.

Deadlines arbitrarily set by one of the parties are in a different category and have different implications. If your opponent tells you that the deal is off unless you accept his terms before a certain date, if an employee threatens to resign unless he is promoted before the end of the year, if a prospective buyer of your house tells you that he will buy another house unless you accept his offer, you're facing a deadline which is entirely negotiable. Time limits come and go. Your opponent's ultimatum might be serious, semi-serious or not serious at all. More often than not, it will be semi-serious. Your opponent is not entirely bluffing, but if he feels that some progress has been made or some hope is given before the deadline expires he is willing, often more than willing, to continue the negotiations although his ultimatum has not been met.

Deadlines can be useful tools in negotiations. They tend to enhance concentration and force decisions. Most headway in negotiations is often made shortly before a deadline. If you sense that your opponent is about to give in, it might be a good tactic to set a deadline in order to force him over the threshold.

Deadlines are also used to make your opponent stop bluffing, deceiving, complaining, threatening or playing games. If your opponent perceives your deadline as real, you might suddenly find a changed person at the other end of the table.

I have already mentioned the impact of deadlines on agendas. They should be a factor in your choice of the sequence in which the issues will be discussed.

Inexperienced negotiators tend to be too aware of their own deadlines and to underestimate those facing their opponent. If you are coping with deadlines which have not been set by your opponent, wonder first of all whether they can be stretched and, second, whether or not your opponent is aware of them. If not, see to it that he remains unaware of them. If your opponent is labouring under his own deadlines, it's a crucial part of your preparations to try to find out about them.

Negotiating abroad

Time is a particularly poignant factor when you are negotiating abroad. In negotiations between parties one of whom has flown in from the other end of the world and will return home at a certain hour on a certain date, the finality of the departure provides for both parties a strict, objective deadline and can, depending on the circumstances and the eagerness of either party to conclude a deal, work two ways. As we have seen, in the majority of cases it's the negotiator who comes in from abroad who feels the pressure. He has travelled a long way, invested a lot of time and incurred huge expenses to take part in the negotiations, and the idea of returning home empty handed is often anathema to him. As a result, he's more anxious to get the deal done than he would have been if he had negotiated at home. And the party with the home advantage is very much aware of that.

Sometimes it works the other way around. I remember negotiations engaged in by the owner of an office building. After many attempts to sell it at home he gave up and decided to look for a buyer abroad. Finally the interest of a foreign investor was aroused sufficiently to make him fly in to negotiate a purchase. The seller thought that the situation would be as usual, that the foreigner would be so eager to conclude a deal before going home that he, the seller, would be in the driver's seat. However, things worked out quite differently.

The foreigner flew in over the weekend and informed the seller straight away that he would leave again the next Friday. The first round of negotiations was scheduled for Monday morning. That meeting was postponed by the visitor at the very last moment because he had been up late at a party the night before. On Monday afternoon he arrived late, elaborated in detail on the meals which he had enjoyed so far, complained about the weather, the coffee and his hotel, turned out to be a master of small talk, in short, did everything but negotiate. At the end of that session, he informed the seller that he had earmarked Tuesday for a visit to relatives and that on Wednesday morning he wanted to play tennis. On Wednesday afternoon he appeared to be ready to negotiate, but still at a snail's pace. In the negotiations of Thursday he proved to be rigid and inflexible. On Friday morning a deal was made. A miserable one from the seller's point of view.

So departure dates, one way or another, loom large in negotiations abroad. That might be a reason to leave your opponent in the dark about your departure date. Beware of your opponent's courteous offer to have his secretary reconfirm your return flight. Courteous he might be, but you can assume that above all he wants to find out when you will return; in other words, to get deadline information. In fact he has possibly already called your hotel to find out for how long your room is booked. Some people go so far as to make a hotel reservation for a shorter or longer period of time than they intend to stay. Conversely, if time works for you, as it did for the foreign investor, do not overlook any opportunity to rub your departure date in.

Some tips on timing

It always amazes me how often people agree unnecessarily to negotiate at a time which is not convenient for them. The decision when to negotiate and for how long should be a joint one. Negotiate only when it suits you. Take even your idiosyncracies into account. If you know that you are not at your best on Monday mornings or on Friday afternoons, schedule your negotiating session accordingly. If you know that you are a basket case any day before 10am, negotiate only later in the day. If you know that you tire easily, insist on short sessions.

Play with time. Use it for tactical purposes. If time is against him, your opponent will probably want to negotiate as often as possible, for as long as possible. In that case, agree only on short sessions with long intervals. Make yourself less available. To increase pressure on your opponent, consider once in a while cancelling at the last moment a meeting which he desperately wanted to have much earlier in the first place. However, do so only within limits – not to the extent of being rude or unreliable.

Time tends to erode aspiration levels. When negotiations drag on for a long time, concentrate on keeping your own aspiration level up and take advantage of the probable erosion of the aspiration level of your opponent.

It's often overlooked that the expiry date of a contract can be of importance and should in that case be a negotiating issue. A union of street cleaners would prefer their collective labour contracts to expire at the start of the summer, when a strike would be felt (and smelled!) much more than in the middle of the winter. On the other hand, some employers are so forward-looking (or wicked) that they consciously try to have labour contracts expire in the middle of the winter, when it will be more difficult to find volunteers for the picket lines.

Time your negotiations so as to put yourself in the driver's seat. A company which is about to go public has to disclose every pending or imminent lawsuit. If you have to settle something with such a company invite it to the negotiating table shortly before it intends to go public. And a central heating repair man is in a better position to negotiate a price before he rescues a customer in the middle of a freeze-up. Favours are the quickest thing forgotten.

Telephone negotiating

Timing goes to the essence of telephone negotiations. Such

negotiations are in two prominent respects different from face-to-face negotiations: the opponents cannot see each other (which is a handicap for negotiators who have a keen eye for non-verbal clues) and the decision when to start the particular round of negotiations is unilaterally taken by one of the parties. The caller takes the initiative. He decides the timing. He will call when he is totally prepared, in the right mood, in no rush at all, after he has gone through his files and over his notes again and after he has had his two coffees. Often he will catch his opponent unawares, in a meeting or when he has other things on his mind.

Do not negotiate over the phone when you are not prepared in every sense of the word — when you are in a meeting, when you could be interrupted at any time, when you are about to leave for the airport or when you just do not feel like negotiating. Take your opponent's call only when you are fully ready for it. Do not hesitate to say that you will call back. And, as a sideline, if you are engaged in telephone negotiations, always have a pretext ready for breaking off the conversation when it suits you. You have to take a call from Timbuktu on the other line but you will call back shortly (read: when you are better prepared, when you have thought about ways to handle the sticky questions your opponent was in the process of asking you or to rebut the tough arguments he was using against you). Such untruths are permissible in the context of negotiations, but if they would bother you, do not give any reason for having to discontinue the conversation. Your opponent might gather that you broke off because your case was breaking apart, but that would not be as bad as continuing negotiations which were going in the wrong direction.

Some Tactics

Even for those negotiators who prefer to abstain from tactics, this chapter is important because they need to be able to recognize tactics when they are used against them and they should be aware of possible counter-measures.

Of course, tactics are of a lesser order than strategy. Strategy determines where you want to go, tactics how you get there. There are no good tactics for the wrong strategy. Before spending time and energy on devising tactics, you must have an overall strategic plan. And your tactics should support your strategy. Short-term tactics should not be used to arrive at a long-term relationship. Win/lose tactics do not make sense in the context of win/win negotiations.

Let's take a look at some specific tactics.

Last-minute escalation

After the deal has in essence been done, one party tries to change it in his favour. Generally just a little, enough to make a difference but not enough to make his opponent walk away from the agreement.

You have negotiated the purchase of a house. After long negotiations, you have agreed a price of £100,000 with the seller. This price is more than you had in mind, in fact a little bit more than you can afford. But nevertheless you're pleased with the purchase. Exchange of contracts will take place in a week. During that week you go over the house with your family, you allocate rooms to your children, you discuss interior decoration with your wife, you buy furniture, you tell your friends about the house. In short, when you arrive at the moment for the exchange of contracts, you have mentally moved already. Then the seller tells you that, although he does not deny that a price of £100,000 has been agreed on, he has changed his mind and wants £101,000. What do you do? On the one hand, you're furious that the seller is trying to change the deal at the very last moment. On the other hand, what is £1,000 on a purchase price of £100,000? You have already agreed to pay more than you should. How could you go home and tell your wife, children and friends that the purchase has fallen through after all?

These tactics are rotten, unethical . . . but often used. Don't apply them yourself. If your opponent does, call his bluff. For the same reason that he expects you to give in (because the extra cost is too insignificant to forgo the transaction), he will almost always drop his last-minute demand as soon as you resist it firmly.

Fading beauty

Your interest was aroused and you were getting hooked by an offer which at first glance looked wonderful but which later on becomes more and more unattractive.

You see an ad in the newspaper about a terrific sale of home computers. The shop is quite far away, but the bargain justifies the trip. When you arrive, the salesman tells you that, unfortunately, you are just too late, the advertised computer is not available any more. But he happens to have other computers, of even better quality. They are not reduced but they are good buys anyway. You have travelled all the way, convinced that you would come home with a new computer. Although in normal circumstances you would not even have considered buying the other computer, you are tempted to do so now. At least you are willing to subject yourself to the sales talk with all the foreseeable consequences.

A financial institution advertises amazingly low interest rates for loans. You arrange a meeting. When you discuss the loan in detail, it appears that the advantages of the low interest rate are largely offset by all kind of charges and fees. If you had known about those extra costs, you would not have gone to this institution. But now that you have got this far, the simplest thing to do is to stay.

A nasty example of these tactics goes as follows. You are called by somebody who wants to buy your business. You're not interested in selling out, in fact you have never even thought about it. The prospective buyer, however, mentions tentatively a very attractive price, let's say £750,000. That changes the picture for you: £750,000 is much more than you ever thought your business would be worth. Although selling still does not really appeal to you, you agree to meet the prospective buyer. The meeting is set for the next week. In the meantime you start to think about everything you could do with all that money. You and your wife discuss the luxuries which selling could bring, from early retirement to the yacht you always dreamed of. When you meet the prospective buyer, you have mentally spent the money already. And then the prospective buyer says something like: 'I realize that I mentioned £750,000 over the phone but we made a mistake, we misunderstood, we miscalculated. I offer you £500,000.' If that amount had been mentioned in the initial phone conversation, you would not have even considered meeting the prospective buyer. But now that both of you are there, what harm could be done by talking? Moreover, during the past week the idea of selling has gradually become very attractive to you. You end up with a deal which would have been completely unacceptable to you only a week before.

These tactics are often applied in international transactions. The further one has travelled, the larger the expense one has incurred, the more one will be inclined to 'work out something', even after the initial beauty of the proposal, which got one on to the plane, has faded.

Last-minute escalation and fading beauty are related to each other. The main difference is in the timing. Last-minute escalation is applied at the very end, fading beauty at the very beginning of negotiations. This makes fading beauty a more acceptable tactic, but not one to be recommended.

How can you defend yourself against fading beauty? Primarily by self-discipline. Force yourself to keep in mind why you were initially interested. Ask yourself whether and why you should remain interested with all these changes for the worse. Would you have bought that home computer for the standard price if you had not been lured into the shop? Would you have accepted the terms of the financial institution's loan if it were not for the fact that you are sitting in their office? Would you have considered selling your business if you had known beforehand that the price would be so much less than what appeared to be the buyer's opening offer? If the answer is no, don't concentrate on your wasted time and your lost illusions. Be rational and walk out.

Good guy/bad guy

You are negotiating against a team of negotiators. One of the negotiators is rigid, unreasonable, unpleasant. But his partner is quite reasonable and pleasant, apparently embarrassed by the behaviour of his colleague. He almost seems to take sides with you. After a while you find it difficult to contradict or disagree with the good guy. You wish to reciprocate. You want to reward him for his reasonableness. Feelings of gratitude start to undermine your bargaining effectiveness.

These tactics are often applied in one form or another. They are very effective and quite legitimate.

The good guy and the bad guy can be the same person: your opponent has been very unpleasant and unreasonable, but suddenly he grows more and more pleasant and reasonable. You start to feel an inclination to reward him for his sudden, unexpected reasonableness. And what better means to do so than by making concessions to him?

The 'bad guy' can also be a third party, like a boss, members, a wife or even an abstraction like a budget or company policy. Your opponent suggests that *he* understands you, that personally he finds your position reasonable, even that he himself would like to agree with you, but that, to his utter regret, he cannot do so because his boss would fire him, his members would not support him, his wife would divorce him, his budget does not allow for it, the policy of his organization is totally against it etc.

Your opponent creates an atmosphere in which *you* are being pressured to solve *his* problem and the only way you can help him is by giving in.

Principles often serve as bad guys. Matters of principle are beyond discussion. Whatever the merits of your proposals, you must understand that your opponent cannot even consider them, because they go against his principles.

The best counter-measure against these tactics is a mental process. Keep it constantly in mind that the good guy is not so good, that he is on the same team as the bad guy, that he conspires with him, that it should not be up to you to solve your opponent's problems, that his problems are probably fictitious anyway, that if he really thinks your position is reasonable, he should explain that to his boss/members/wife, that neither budgets nor policies are cast in concrete, that principles are often invoked when arguments fail.

Good guy/bad guy can be a good approach when you negotiate with a team and want to find out if a combative attitude will be effective. Keep one member of the team initially in the background. If the fighting approach does not work and you want to switch over to a more co-operative mode, use the untarnished team member to change the atmosphere.

Take it or leave it

Famous last words, which more often than not are not the last at all!
Frequently they are used prematurely or frivolously. However, they
can be appropriate in the right circumstances. What are these?

The first requirement is that you should be serious, you should
mean what you are saying, you should be able and willing to live with
the risk of your opponent deciding to leave it. You lose tremendous
credibility if you have to come back on a 'take it or leave it. You must
therefore be quite sure that the chances of your opponent taking it are
good. If that's not the case, the risk that you end up with a deadlock
which requires you to take back your 'take it or leave it' is
considerable.

Never use this approach early in negotiations. Otherwise you give
the impression that you prefer dictating to negotiating (a very human
urge, by the way; what a pity that most opponents, also human
beings, often have the same urge!).

It is of crucial importance never to use the words themselves. They
sound abrasive and arrogant. They almost invite a 'leave it'. We have
seen before that most messages can be phrased in different ways and
that unpleasant news is best relayed in a friendly and reasonable
manner. Keep that very well in mind when you resort to 'take it or
leave it'.

In order to make it easier for the opponent to stomach your 'take it
or leave it', also be willing to soften the message by extensive
explanation. 'Take it or leave it' should not mean that you're not
willing to talk any further. You're perfectly willing to continue the
discussion. You're only not willing to better the deal for your
opponent.

Although you should be serious when you say 'take it or leave it',
it's often wise to have a final-final offer as a back-up to your final offer.
A relatively minor concession after a 'take it or leave it' does not
necessarily infringe your credibility.

It's difficult to generalize about how to counter a 'take it or leave it'.
I recommend, however, always to test it. Although 'take it or leave it'
should not be used rashly, that's exactly what happens a lot. A 'take it
or leave it' is often at least somewhat flexible. One way to test it is to
ignore it. Continue to negotiate as if you have not heard or understood
the message. Sometimes it is smart to play dumb.

You can also take the position that you do not wish to negotiate on
the basis of a 'take it or leave it'. If you wish, make it a matter of
principle. But be prepared for the risk that if your opponent is serious,

there will be a deadlock.

You can also try to move the negotiations onto a different track. Modify the deal. When your opponent offers a price on a 'take it or leave it' basis, throw out some 'what ifs'. What if the quantities were larger or smaller? What if the quality were improved? What if delivery were speeded up? What if there were 60 days' credit instead of 30?

Always leave your opponent a face-saving way out of a 'take it or leave it'. Again, too many opponents try a 'take it or leave it' frivolously. When they realize that it doesn't work, they would love to eat their words. You have to make that possible for them.

Although you should not resort to a 'take it or leave it' early in negotiations, a special brand of it, 'first offer, final offer', goes even further: the initial offer is being submitted on a 'take it or leave it' basis.

The advantages are clear. You take the initiative totally. Your opponent is on the defensive. If it works, the negotiations will be simple and short.

The risks, however, are overwhelming. You appear arrogant. It is psychologically almost impossible for your opponent to accept on the spot and, if he does, he will do so reluctantly and only because he feels that he has no choice. Another disadvantage is that if you have to retreat from a first and final offer your loss of face is devastating. And last but not least, your first and final offer might exceed what could have been obtained by negotiating. With the benefit of hindsight you might have been too generous. Because it has to be borne in mind that a first and final offer only has a chance of being accepted if it is also fair and reasonable from the opponent's point of view. That means that you must have a good idea about what will be acceptable and fair to him. But, being forced to be reasonable and fair, you might go too far and offer more than would have been necessary.

I don't like 'first offer, final offer' at all. I have never seen it work and I would say don't use it, especially not in public negotiations or in a case in which your opponent has to account to other people. You should not put an opponent into the position of having to tell his people that, as far as he is concerned, the negotiations consisted only of saying 'yes, yes, yes'. Nevertheless, the only instance I know of in which this approach seemed to work for a while concerned public negotiations. In America in the late nineteen-forties, General Electric presented in its collective labour contract negotiations its proposals to the union on a non-negotiable basis. In fact, this approach is often called 'Boulwareism' after General Electric's former Vice President for Industrial Affairs, James Bouleware. For many years, General

Electric got away with this approach. However, the first time it did not work, a long and bitter strike ensued. I assume, by the way, that General Electric used this approach not merely as bargaining tactics but also as a way to convey to its employees that they did not need their union to get a fair and reasonable offer from the company.

One way to counter a first and final offer is to submit your opening offer on the same basis. The result will be an immediate deadlock. Your opponent prefers dictating over negotiating. Well, so do you. He will not let you dictate the deal. Neither will you let him. You force your opponent into a position of either forgoing an agreement or having to start negotiating seriously.

I said previously that 'take it or leave it – first offer, final offer' is an unusual approach. But, come to think of it, is that true? Isn't a price tag a subtle but commonplace form of a first and final offer? The store wants to sell, you want to buy. So you have to negotiate about the price. The store cuts the negotiations short by saying: 'this is our offer, the price is non-negotiable, it's our first offer but at the same time our final offer'. Also, menus, price-lists, car rental agreements, standard leases etc are in practice first and final offers. In theory you could try to discuss with a car rental company the terms of their agreement but for practical reasons they could not think of negotiating. They would have to expand their force of employees tenfold if they were to open the door to customers negotiating the conditions of each and every rental. But if you were to consider renting a hundred cars for a lengthy period of time, the company would gladly be willing to deviate from its standard agreement, in other words, to negotiate the terms of the lease. And in some shops, price tags are negotiable. In many countries, Mexico for example, a price tag is generally just an extreme opening position leaving ample room for negotiations.

Limited authority

Frequently a negotiator can only accept an agreement subject to approval by somebody else, whether it is his boss, his members, the full board etc. Quite often, however, a negotiator suggests for tactical purposes that he has less authority than he really has. This provides him with an opportunity to reconsider, to backtrack, to return with new demands. It also makes it easier for him to be rigid. Whatever he personally thinks of your demands, whichever concessions he would personally be inclined to make, he just does not have the authority to accommodate you.

Psychologically you're in a very uncomfortable position. You do not know to whom you are really talking. There's almost a screen between you and the person you want to influence. You do not only have to convince the person who is there, but much more his invisible, far-away principal.

Understating the negotiating authority often goes arm in arm with last-minute escalation. Your opponent consents to a deal, subject to approval by his boss. Later he returns with the message that his boss has approved the deal, but, just as you draw a breath of relief, he adds, 'provided that one or two minor matters are changed'. To the advantage of the opponent, of course. Remember what to do when an opponent applies last-minute escalation against you. Do not give in. Call his bluff. Generally he just tries.

Another limited-authority ploy goes as follows. The higher authority which has to approve the transaction, is suddenly gone and incommunicado. His people suggest that they are desperately trying to get in touch with him, but in reality they are only busy finding out whether they can make a better deal with a third party. And the deal they made with you serves as a floor for them in those negotiations. Or they play this game to test your eagerness to conclude the deal. If you respond by calling five times a day to enquire whether the missing man has been found, it's obvious that you want the deal very much and that you are probably willing to make further concessions. Or, if a deadline is confronting you, they may be stalling for time in order to renegotiate the deal when the deadline is breathing down your neck.

In essence your opponent is getting himself a free option. You are basically committed but he has the time to reconsider, to negotiate with other parties etc.

Be suspicious when somebody suddenly cannot be found at all. As a counter-measure you can attach a time limit to your willingness to conclude the deal as negotiated. If the missing boss remains missing, the deal is off. Or you can inform your opponent that, as long as his boss does not show up, you feel free to negotiate with somebody else.

Always make sure before negotiations start what authority your opponent has. Try to avoid negotiating with more authority than he has. If he has limited authority, limit your authority accordingly. Tell him that everything you offer, concede or accept is contingent on him getting the deal fully approved. While you are negotiating, keep it in mind at all times that when ratification is required, there is no agreement before the deal has been approved and that ratification may require further concessions. If the authority of your opponent is too limited for meaningful negotiations, refuse to negotiate with him and insist on meeting face-to-face with someone who has at least substantial authority.

Lock-in

One party makes it impossible for himself to yield. He locks himself into an immovable position from which there's no retreat, even if he would like there to be. He deliberately deprives himself of the manoeuvring room necessary to make concessions. And by letting the other party know — which is essential — how locked-in he is, he assumes that the other party will give up hope and not make any attempt to obtain concessions from him. Paradoxically, he hopes to strengthen his bargaining position by giving up control over the situation.

The classic example is a theoretical one. Two cars meet on a single lane road. A collision can only be avoided if one of them drives onto the shoulder of the road. Both of them want and expect the other one to do so. But then one driver pulls his steering wheel off and throws it out of the window. Now his 'opponent' has no choice anymore. The driver who deprived himself of steering ability has no longer the power to avoid a collision by driving onto the shoulder, even if on reflection that's what he would prefer to do. All room for negotiating has been removed. Realistically speaking, only one decision is possible. As much as he hates to do so, the other driver has to leave the road.

There are more real-life examples than there should be. The politician who again and again publicly announces that he will never join forces with a certain opponent unless those and those conditions are met. Doing so he raises firm expectations among his supporters. And, later on, when he is negotiating with his opponent he will use those expectations as a reason why he cannot even consider giving in. The union leader who, before the start of collective labour contract negotiations, assures his members that under no circumstances will he yield on those and those points and later on advises management that, whatever his own opinion, his members will simply not allow him to concede those points. The management of the company subject to a take-over bid which, through newspaper ads and press releases, slashes out at the acquiring company, attacking the integrity and competence of its president, denigrating the bid, in short, putting itself in a corner from which retreat is hard even if, on reflection, it comes to the conclusion that the best interest of the shareholders requires acceptance of the bid.

Come to think of it, did not the Sibyl of Cumae apply some kind of lock-in tactics when she tried to sell nine Sibylline Books (the Libri Sibyllini) to Tarquinius Priscus of Rome? After Tarquinius told her that he considered the asking price for the nine books unacceptably high, she threw three of them into the fire and asked the same price for the remaining six. When Tarquinius told her that asking the same price for fewer goods did not seem quite logical to him, she hurled another three in the fire, keeping the same price again, although only three books were left. Whereupon Tarquinius threw in the towel, yielded to those brazen lock-in tactics and agreed to pay for the remaining three books the very amount which the Sibyl of Cumae had initially asked for the entire set of nine. (Does the fact that those three remaining tomes were destroyed by fire sometime thereafter indicate that lock-in tactics should never be yielded to?)

The problem with these tactics is primarily that they are often used by inept negotiators who have not thought through the consequences. There might be circumstances in which an experienced, able negotiator concludes that the potential benefits of these tactics justify the ever-present risks. But more often than not it is the inexperienced negotiator who deprives himself of manoeuvring room. Quite often he does so inadvertently. In the heat of a political speech or the excitement of a union meeting, perhaps when he is involved in a fight or contest and hopes that by making promises and raising expectations he will gain the upper hand, he gradually slips into the trap of locking himself in.

Lock-in tactics look like but are quite different from negotiating by choice with very limited authority. In both instances the negotiator lacks much manoeuvring room. And in both instances he has for tactical reasons elected to be in that position. But the use of lock-in tactics is pretty final. Getting out is either impossible or only possible at a severe cost. A voluntarily restricted mandate, on the other hand, can always be broadened if it proves to be too much of a straitjacket.

What to do when the opponent has locked himself in? If he is really locked in you might not have much choice. But lock-ins are frequently not absolute. By retreating, your opponent may lose face or the confidence of his supporters or members, but that is his problem. If he (or his constituency) wants the deal badly enough, he will after all probably prefer a get-out to an impasse.

Moreover, it is essential to these tactics that the lock-in has been communicated to and understood by the opponent. They wouldn't work if, in the theoretical example, the driver had not noticed that the other one had thrown away his wheel. Neither can management be influenced if it is not aware of the high expectations which the union leaders have raised. So you can also pretend that you are not aware of the immovable position your opponent has chosen to be in. And if he tries to explain to you what position he's in, you may try to suggest that you don't understand why he cannot retreat if he wants to. Another example of being smart by playing dumb. But always take the position that the lock-in is his problem. He elected to lock himself in. It is not up to you to let him out.

'Pardon my French'

Never negotiate in a language which you do not speak fluently. There is no greater disadvantage than having to talk, react, think, be smart, creative, persuasive, exude self-confidence and competence in a language with which you don't feel entirely comfortable.

However, it can be to your tactical advantage to negotiate in a language which is not your native one, but which you speak effortlessly. A language which essentially you speak as your own except maybe (and for these tactics even preferably) for the pronunciation. Pleading that you are speaking a language which is not your own enables you to ask your opponent to repeat thorny questions (so that you have more time to think up a good answer) or even to backtrack on a commitment ('sorry, I misunderstood', 'that is not what I meant' etc).

I used this ploy recently when I was selling a painting to an art dealer in France. I did not know much about the painting and I assumed that the art dealer would ask me many questions to test my knowledge about paintings in general and this painting in particular. That's exactly what he did. Although my French is quite reasonable I stammered and stuttered each time I was asked something. Soon he gave up. He might not have been impressed by my knowledge of the French language, but neither did he find out about my lack of knowledge about the painting. There remains of course the fact that, in violation of my own sermons, I was ill-prepared for the negotiations.

The other way around, if you are convinced that somebody is understating his knowledge of the language which is being used at the negotiating table, point out that you are aware of what he is doing. Incidentally, this is in general a good method to counter the use of tactics which you find disagreeable. If you say something like 'Listen

John, let's call a spade a spade, you're trying to apply such and such tactics against me and I resent it', John will probably discontinue those tactics immediately.

In an extreme case you should insist that your opponent uses an interpreter, although that would also place him in a somewhat advantageous position. Assuming that in reality he understands the language you are speaking well enough, he now has ample time to prepare a reaction to something you say and each time he has spoken, he can concentrate on observing you while you are listening to the interpreter. Furthermore, for somebody who is not used to it, having an interpreter involved is often confusing and distracting.

So you have to choose between two evils when your opponent deliberately understates his knowledge of the language used for the negotiations and continues to do so after you have urged him to stop. You either subject yourself to the disadvantages of having an interpreter involved or you give the opponent the chance to proceed with this ploy. However, in win/win negotiations you should seriously consider breaking off the negotiations. All indications are that your opponent is not the right partner to do business with.

Intimidation

I call forms of misbehaviour such as abuse, intimidation and rudeness tactics because it is often for tactical reasons that people misbehave in the course of negotiations. Common examples: your opponent lets you wait for an outrageously long time, he makes you sit in an uncomfortable chair or a chair which is lower than his own, he is belligerent, he treats you with contempt, he insults you.

Never ever accept poor treatment. Most probably your opponent is testing you, checking how far he can go and he will go as far as you let him. Be assertive. Protest in no uncertain terms. However, also be aware of the opposite of these tactics. Opponents who are too charming, too cajoling, too suave, too understanding, too co-operative. The chances are that you are being seduced and seduction often leads to something you may later regret: in this instance, you may be saddled with a lousy agreement.

Incidentally, a good way to make people think twice before letting you wait too long is to use their phone – for long distance or, even better, international calls. You want to be shown in promptly? Pick up the phone and start to talk Japanese!

Emotional outbursts

Controlled anger can, as we have seen, be an effective way to signal to your opponent that he has gone as far as he can go, that your bottom line has been reached, that he should stop here and now. But let your anger be controlled. Spontaneous emotional outbursts are generally ineffective and counter-productive, although it is very difficult to handle somebody who suddenly bursts into tears or otherwise acts irrationally.

What are good counter-measures? Against real emotional out-bursts: do not react, keep cool, let your opponent rage. Generally he reveals in a rage more information than he should. Against controlled, simulated emotional outbursts: do not be intimidated, make a joke, make it clear to your opponent that you are not impressed.

Advance man

In American campaigns election advance men are used by political candidates for scouting and reconnaisance, to test the water and gather information on opponents. Regrettably they are also sometimes used for negotiations.

Information from heaven

At the end of a negotiating round your opponent leaves behind, seemingly by mistake but in fact on purpose, notes or documents. You cannot resist the impulse to read them and you find the information most interesting and useful. Well, interesting as that information might be, it is far from being useful. It's erroneous and left behind in order to mislead you, for example, about offers which have supposedly been received from third parties or about your opponent's bottom line. As a variant of this silly trick, which is fortunately not used a lot, your opponent could also take his notes in such a way that you can read them. Once again, he wants you to because they are misleading.

When I call this trick 'silly' I should bear in mind that it was supposedly often used by the not so silly American financial wizard Bernard Baruch, although not in negotiations (at least not in negotiations in which he was face to face with the other party).

Legend has it that when he was about to buy shares in company XYZ, Baruch used to scribble notes feverishly to himself while he was travelling by train. Striding down from the train he managed to drop his notes. Other passengers, knowing his reputation, jumped on them, and read something like 'On arrival in the office: sell immediately 10,000 shares XYZ short'. Wall Street being Wall Street, word that Baruch was about to short XYZ heavily got round fast. And as soon as this rumour had driven the price of XYZ down far enough, Baruch placed his buying order.

How can you defend yourself against this trick? First of all by being honest yourself. It's hard to cheat an honourable person! Do not read the documents which he left, do not glance at his notes. In fact, his trickiness in leaving the misleading stuff is being equalled by your dishonesty in jumping at the opportunity to get inside information. In any case, when you get information in this or any other suspicious manner, be cautious with it. Proceed on the basis that the information might, but also might not, be true and in any case has to be verified.

Conclusion

In an article about a certain American politician the *International Herald Tribune* (19 November 1986) raised the question of what makes the man tick and answers: 'Not just budgets and taxes, but the dynamic that produces them: that process of listening, talking, winning trust, testing, advancing, retreating, cajoling, bluffing, waiting, massaging, synthesizing, failing, splitting the difference, trying again, compromising and sometimes getting there.' Isn't that a marvellous, colourful, wide-ranging (although somewhat over-romanticized) description of what negotiating is all about? I do not know whether the subject of the article is a good politician. I do not even know whether he's a good negotiator, but one thing I do know; he *loves* negotiating. If he ever wrote a book about negotiating he would probably call it *The Joy of Negotiating*.

Let me make one final and important point: negotiating is not frightfully difficult, it does not require an awesome degree of intelligence, smartness and sang-froid, it is not something only intellectual prima donnas should indulge in.

This book should make the reader a better negotiator, I have said. Some people would disagree with this statement. They take the position that the art of negotiating cannot be taught and cannot be learned. They believe that one either has or has not the qualities required for effective negotiating and that successful negotiators are born not made. At first glance Chapter 1 may support this belief. Not everyone is patient, lacks the need to be liked, is able to handle rejections, can listen and observe, and can keep a tight rein on his emotions.

Nevertheless I'm convinced that anyone can acquire some negotiating skills.

First of all, everyone has within himself some room for manoeuvring and improvement and everyone is to some extent able to rise above himself. A naturally impatient person can probably not turn himself into a classic example of patience, but if he realizes how great a handicap impatience is for a negotiator, and understands why that is the case, he can force himself to remain patient during negotiations.

If you know that a negotiator often ends up with the short stick because he gave up too quickly, you can tell yourself something like: 'I know that I tend to give up after two rejections — in negotiations I cannot afford to do — tomorrow I will not yield before my opponent has said "no" at least four times'.' If you understand the importance of listening and observing you can make a conscious effort to listen and observe better than you tend to do naturally, for example by silently repeating to yourself what the opponent is saying and 'reporting' to yourself what you are observing. And there are many tricks for restraining one's emotions, for example counting till 10 (or to 50 if one is really upset, but then one might not be able to reach 50) before reacting.

So, if you know what's required for a good negotiator, understand the reasons why, have the proper motivation and a normal dose of self-discipline, you can turn yourself into a better negotiator than you are by nature, in fact a better negotiator than you ever thought you could be.

Moreover, many fundamental principles of good negotiating can be taught and learned. The outcome of negotiations is to a large extent determined by the degree to which the negotiators were well prepared. And preparation is a prime example of a negotiating skill which has hardly anything to do with natural ability and can be acquired by almost anybody. The same is true of concession-making, another pivotal part of negotiating. Everyone who manages to stick to the 20 or so do's and don'ts in this area is a greatly improved negotiator. Likewise nobody should think that great mysteries are involved in avoiding or breaking deadlocks. Learn and use an handful of rather simple and obvious methods and rules: that's as mysterious as it gets. And while applying certain tactics might not be equally easy for everybody, it all starts with knowing which tactics there are to apply, which circumstances lend themselves to their application and which potential benefits and dangers each of them entails. That knowledge can be obtained by everybody who wants it.

Although it helps to have been born with many of the traits useful for good negotiating, I'm firmly convinced that skilful negotiators are not born but made. Self-made, that is.

Bibliography

Acheson, Dean: *Power and Diplomacy*, Harvard University Press, 1958.

Argyle, Michael: *The Psychology of Interpersonal Behaviour*, Pelican, 1967.

Bacharach, SB and Lawler, EJ: *Bargaining: Power Tactics and Outcomes*, Jossey Bass, San Francisco, 1981.

Bartos, OJ: *Process and Outcomes of Negotiations*, Columbia University Press, 1974.

Bigoness, WJ: 'The impact of initial bargaining position and alternative modes of third party intervention in resolving bargaining impasses', *Organizational Behavior and Human Performance*, 1976, 17, 185–198.

Blaker, Michael: *Japanese International Negotiating Style*, Columbia University Press, 1977.

Bosmajian, Haig A: *The Rhetoric of Nonverbal Communication*, Scott, Foresman and Co, Glenview, Illinois.

Brock, J: *Bargaining Beyond Impasse*, Auburn House, Boston, 1982.

Callières, François de: *De la Manière de Négocier avec les Souverains*, Mercure Galant, 1716.

Carnevale, PJD, Pruitt DG and Britton, SD: 'Looking tough: the negotiator under constituent surveillance', *Personality and Social Psychology Bulletin*, 1979, 5, 118–121.

Carnevale, PJD, Sherer, P and Pruitt, DG: 'Some determinants of concession rate and distributive tactics in negotiation', Paper presented at the 87th annual convention of the American Psychological Association, New York, September 1979.

Coddington, Alan: *Theories of the Bargaining Process*, Aldine, New York, 1968.

Cox, Archibald and Dunlop, John T: 'The duty to bargain collectively during the term of an existing agreement', *Harvard Law Review*, 63, 1097–1133 (May 1950).

Craig, Gordon: 'Techniques of Negotiation', in Ivo J Lederer (ed), *Russian Foreign Policy, Essays in Historical Perspective*, Yale University Press, 1962, pp 351–373.

Critchley, MacDonald: *Silent Language*, Butterworths, London.

Douglas, Ann: 'What can research tell us about mediation', *Labor Law Journal*, 6, 545–552 (August 1955).

Downing, Thomas G: 'Strategy and tactics at the bargaining table', *Personnel*, January-February 1960, pp 58–63.

Dupont, C: *La Négociation: Conduite, Théorie, Applications*, Dalloz, 1982.

Fisher, R, Ury, W: *Getting to Yes*, Houghton Mifflin, Boston, 1981.

Froman, LA Jr, and Cohen, MD: 'Threats and bargaining efficiency', *Behavioral Science*, 1969, 14, 147–153.

Gulliver, PH: *Disputes and Negotiations: A Cross-cultural Perspective*, Academic Press, New York, 1979.

Hamner, WC and Harnett, DL: 'The effects of information and aspiration level on bargaining behaviour', *Journal of Experimental Social Psychology*, 1975, 11, 329–342.

Harnett, DL, Cummings, LL and Hamner, WC: 'Personality, bargaining style, and payoff in bilateral monopoly bargaining among European managers', *Sociometry*, 1973, 36, 325–345.

Harnett, DL, Cummings, LL and Hughes GD: 'The influence of risk-taking propensity on bargaining behavior', *Behavioral Science*, 1968, 13, 91–101.

Iklé, Fred Ch: *How Nations Negotiate*, Harper and Row, New York, 1964.

Jandt, Frea E: *Win-Win Negotiating*, John Wiley & Sons, New York, 1985.

Karrass, CL: *The Negotiating Game*, World Publishing Co, 1968.

Karrass, CL: *Give and Take*, World Publishing Co, 1974.

Kennedy, Gavin: *Everything is Negotiable*, Arrow Books, London, 1982.

Key, Mary Ritchie: *Nonverbal Communication Today*, Mouton, New York.

Komorita, SS: 'Concession-making and conflict resolution', *Journal of Conflict Resolution*, 1973, 17, 745–762.

Komorita, SS: 'Negotiation from strength and the concept of bargaining strength', *Journal of the Theory of Social Behavior*, 1977, 7, 65–79.

Komorita, SS and Esser, JK: 'Frequency of reciprocated concessions in bargaining', *Journal of Personality and Social Psychology*, 1975, 32, 699–705.

Lall, Arthur: *How Communist China Negotiates*, Columbia University Press, 1968.

Marsh, PDV: *Contract Negotiation Handbook*, 2nd edn, Gower, 1984.

Morley, IE and Stephenson, JM: *The Social Psychology of Bargaining*, Allen & Unwin, London, 1977.

Nierenberg, GI: *Fundamentals of Negotiating*, Hawton, New York, 1973.

Peters, Edward: *Strategy and Tactics in Labor Negotiations*, National Foreman's Institute, Inc, New London, 1955.

Pruitt, DG, Drews, JL: 'The effect of time pressure, time elapsed and the opponents concession rate on behaviour in negotiation', *Journal of Experimental Social Psychology*, 1969, 43–60.

Pruitt, DG: 'Power and bargaining' in B Seidenberg and A Snadowsky (eds), *Social Psychology: An Introduction*, Free Press, New York, 1976.

Pruitt, DG: *Negotiation Behaviour*, Academic Press, London, 1981.

Raiffa, H: *The Art and Science of Negotiation*, Harvard University Press, 1982.

Ryder, MS: 'Strategy in collective bargaining negotiations', *Labor Law Journal*, 7:353–358 (June 1956).

Schelling, TC: *The Strategy of Conflict*, Harvard University Press, 1960.

Scott, WP: *The Skills of Negotiating*, Gower, 1981.

Shea, Gordon F: *Creative Negotiating*, CBI Publishing Co, Boston, 1983.

Siegel, Sidney, and Fouraker, Lawrence E: *Bargaining and Group Decision Making*, McGraw-Hill, New York, 1960.

Sparks, Donald B: *The Dynamics of Effective Negotiation*, Gulf Publishing Co, Houston, 1982.

Sperber, Philip: *Fail-Safe Business Negotiating*, Prentice-Hall, Englewood Cliffs, 1983.

Stevens, Carl M: 'On the theory of negotiation', *Quarterly Journal of Economics*, 72, 77–97 (February 1958).

Stevens, Carl M: *Strategy and Collective Bargaining Negotiation*, McGraw-Hill, New York, 1963.

Strauss, A: *Negotiations: Varieties, Contexts, Processes and Social Order*, Jossey Bass, San Francisco, 1978.

Tornatzky, L and Giewitz, PJ: 'The effects of threat and attraction on interpersonal bargaining', *Psychonomic Science*, 1968, 13, 125–126.

Young, PR (ed): *Bargaining: Formal Theories of Negotiation*, University of Illinois Press, 1975.

Zartman, W and Berman, MR: *The Practical Negotiator*, Yale University Press, 1982.

Index

acceptance time 24–5
advance man 81
agenda 20, 45–7, 65
agreement 25–6, 36, 42–3, 48, 76
  compliance with 34–5
  enforcement of 34–5
  necessity for 31–2
anger 81
apology 40, 54
arguments 43, 44
Art and Science of Negotiation (Raiffa) 20
aspirations 49–51, 56, 67
auction-trap 41
authority 19, 21, 45, 75–7
  limited 45, 75–7

balance of power 12
bargaining 25, 75
bargaining position 37, 48, 77
Baruch, Bernard 81–2
best alternative 42–3, 48
bluffing 25, 65, 76
'Boulwareism' 74
break in negotiations 60
brinkmanship 59

certainty 14
checklists 29–30, 36, 47–8
commercial negotiations 12
concessions 17, 50–51, 63, 72
  contingent 53
  cost of 43–5
  final 41
  free 53
  inexpensive valuable 43–4
  making 21, 25–7, 34, 52–7, 84
  mediated 61
  obtaining 54, 77
  patterns of 56, 57
  unnecessary 11, 47
consensus, 21, 23, 30

counter-arguments 43
counter-concessions 17
creativity 12
credibility 55, 59, 73

deadlines 14, 21, 36, 64–5, 76
  and agenda 46
  arbitrary 64, 65
  objective 64, 65
deadlocks 12–13, 21, 59–62, 73, 74
  avoiding 12, 84
  breaking 12, 61, 84
debates 22
departure date 66
devil's advocate 47
dialogue 22
dictating 73, 75
dilemmas of negotiators 18–20
distrust 13
doorknob price 41
draft agreements 27
dry runs 47–8

emotions 14, 26, 81, 83–4
emphasis 23–4

face loss 59, 74, 78
face-saving 74
fact-finding 37–9
fading beauty 70–71
fall-back position 48
final offer 73–5
first offer 50–52, 74–5
'first offer, final offer' 74–5
flexibility 12, 13

give and take 17
goals of negotiation 12, 13, 17, 22, 45, 49
ground rules 20

impasse 19, 60–62

impatience 11, 83, 84
implementation phase, 35, 55
information 17, 19, 36–8, 81, 82
international transactions 71
interpreter 80
interrupting 23
intimidation 80
inventiveness 12
issues 40, 46

Japan 35, 39, 47

Karrass, Chester 24
knock-on effects 33

labour contract negotiations 33, 54, 64, 74, 77
language of negotiation 79–80
last-minute escalation 69–71, 76
'last offer, best offer' 61–2
listening 12, 22–3, 84
litigation 35, 64
lock-in tactics 77–9
lying 17–18

manoeuvring room 78
mediator 61
mind-reading 18
minimum settling point 41
mistrust 19
monitoring 21

negotiating process 17–27; *see also* negotiations
    conclusion 25
    crisis phase 21
    nature 22–5
    orientation phase 20–21
    ratification phase 21
    sessions 20–21
    settlement phase 21
    stages 20–21
negotiating teams 45, 61, 71, 72
negotiations: *see also* negotiating process
    abroad 65–6
    bilateral 32
    definition 17
    internal 32–3
    kinds of 12, 30
    multilateral 32
    private 34
    public 34
    purpose 17
    win/lose 30–31, 64
    win/win 30–31, 64, 80
negotiators 11–15

flawed 11, 13–14
    ideal 15
    qualities 11–13, 83
non-verbal messages 12, 26

observation 12, 84
opening move 27
opening position 40–41, 51

patience 11–12, 15, 84
perseverance 11, 12
persuasion 22
Philips, Frits 23
positions 26–7
power 12, 18
precedents 25, 33
preparation for negotiations 12, 20, 29–48, 79, 84
    checklist 29–30, 36–7, 47–8
presentation 22–3
price tags 75
principles 72, 73, 84

quasi-concessions 55
questions 24

ratification 33, 76
reasonableness 13, 71–2
renegotiation 21, 55–6
review of past negotiations 39
rhetoric 21
rush deals 64

scepticism 13
seduction 80
self-confidence 18
self-control 12
self-criticism 14
self-discipline 84
self-evaluation 19, 25
self-knowledge 14
seminars 49, 52
splitting the difference 55
strategy 45–7, 69
strengths 44

tactics 45–7, 69–82, 84
    advance man 81
    emotional outbursts 81
    fading beauty 70–71
    good guy/bad guy 71–2
    information from heaven 81
    intimidation 80
    last minute escalation 69–70
    limited authority 75–7
    lock-in 77–9

'pardon my French' 79–80
    'take it or leave it' 73–5
'take it or leave it' 73–5
targets 40, 49, 63
telephone negotiations 67–8
time 63–8
    constraints 18
    pressures 36, 63–4
timing 67

trade unions 33, 54, 74–5, 78, 79
trust 19

uncertainty 14, 18, 20
unreasonableness 12, 13, 71–2

walk-away point 40–42
weaknesses 44